:IONS
GOTT

ters

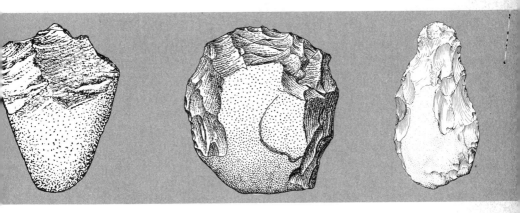

THE STONE

London

AGE HUNTERS

Grahame Clark

Thames and Hudson

CONTENTS

GENERAL EDITOR'S PREFACE

When, from the Renaissance onwards, Western man began to speculate about his ultimate physical and social origins, he could turn only to ancient literary sources, Biblical or Classical, or to the reports of voyagers to the Americas who had there encountered what looked like Primitive Man himself. From the combined evidence, alas, a gloomy picture was constructed, with our earliest ancestors usually defined by a series of negatives – they had 'no culture of the earth; no navigation . . . no account of time; no arts; no letters; no society; and which is worst of all, continual fear, and danger of violent death; and the life of man, solitary, poor, nasty, brutish and short'. This famous passage by Thomas Hobbes, published in 1651, was echoed in almost every writer of that time and later who touched on the origins of human society, and if sometimes the romantic image was imposed on ancient or contemporary primitive peoples, whatever the quality of the nobility of the Noble Savage, there could be no doubt about his savagery.

The origin of man was from the first an uneasy subject to discuss. There was not only the potential clash with the Biblical narrative, but there were ethical and social questions posed as soon as one moved from man as an individual to man as a member of society. The study of the first of these aspects progressed more rapidly than the second, with the development of palaeontology and general vertebrate taxonomy from the end of the eighteenth century onwards. Any examination of the earliest forms of human society however had to wait for the development of precise scientific methods in archaeological field-work and interpretation, and in the absence or ignorance of these a long series of wholly theoretical developmental schemes were put forward from the seventeenth century onwards, to survive today in the Morgan–Engels–Marx assumed sequence of types of human society.

Today the study of our earliest ancestors has come to be one of the most complex departments of prehistoric archaeology, involving a more than usually elaborate interdisciplinary approach. Prehistorians, geologists, palaeontologists, human anatomists, palaeobotanists – the list could be prolonged almost indefinitely – all combine in this exacting field of research, with the result that the evolution of the primates and the inferred structure of man's earliest societies is no longer a matter of supposition and guesswork, however many uncertainties and dubieties still exist. We may agree with Hobbes that the first human communities had 'no culture of the earth' (until ten thousand or so years ago), and 'no navigation' directly attested by archaeological means until about the same time, but the accomplished symmetry and precision of flaking in a hand-axe, let alone the later paintings and carvings of Advanced Palaeolithic peoples from Iberia to the Urals, make 'no arts' a somewhat ridiculous phrase.

From the purely hypothetical ancient savages of Hobbes' time, and before and after it, we have come to recognize that the earliest human communities were those of hunters and food-gatherers whose economies must have been elaborately adjusted to varied natural conditions over enormous areas of the Old World. Their material culture has survived virtually only in so far as it involved substances resistant to decay, such as stone, bone or ivory: we know of two wooden spears however, and though hunters on the move must travel light, one should not forget the likelihood of equipment in fibre, bast, bark, leaves, canes and withies which has failed to survive.

Once we move into the point of time when modern man, *Homo sapiens*, emerges, we are immediately aware of an accelerating tempo of development, quite likely, as Professor Clark points out, to be associated with enlarged capabilities of articulate speech and the formation of verbal concepts. With increased conceptualization the art of Advanced Palaeolithic peoples would find an appropriate situation for its appearance. We have here a new human skill, an extension of the craftsmanship of the maker of tools in stone or bone arising to satisfy new psychological needs which now made urgent claims, and with it, a new member of society:

'the Master of the Venus
whose man-hands god-handled the Willendorf stone
before they unbound the last glaciation . . .
But already he's at it
the form-making proto-maker
busy at the fecund image of her'.

And from the fecund images of the Gravettian culture to the magic mural art of the animals in the caves: 'how they do, within' (to quote David Jones again) 'in an unbloody manner, under the forms of brown haematite and black manganese on the graved lime-face, what is done, without, far on the windy tundra'. Palaeolithic art is now under a new scrutiny, and a new series of interpretations are being put forward, necessarily as subjective, and as much framed within a contemporary psychological climate, as were their predecessors, but with the validity of contemporaneity.

It was the discovery of the American Indians that first prepared the European mind for the recognition of ancient societies of comparable status. In the last century ethnographical 'parallels' were widely employed in discussions on early man, but too frequently without adequate critical control. As a result the whole idea tended to become discredited, and a process of comparison which could in fact be valid and illuminating became suspect, and so was ignored. In this book Professor Clark returns to this theme and shows how a study of surviving or recently surviving peoples with a hunting economy can in fact convey to us precious information on at least some of the types of life our earlier Palaeolithic ancestors could have lived. Such knowledge, by directing our minds towards approaches more humanly relevant than, for instance, an exclusive concentration on the abstract typology of stone tools, should enable us to attack the problems of the most ancient past of man with new understanding.

STUART PIGGOTT

INTRODUCTION

When I undertook this volume I did so in the hope that a more generous allowance of space and illustration would allow me to present a more adequate picture of the early prehistory of man in the Old World than I was able to manage in my chapter of *The Dawn of Civilization*. I also welcomed the opportunity of taking account of new discoveries and above all of a number of major re-appraisals of long-established facts bearing on problems of broad relevance to prehistory. I was also happy that the publishers were willing to forego the coloured reconstructions of prehistoric life featured in the large volume and to include in their place some unposed photographs of living peoples whose way of life most closely resembles that of which the archaeological fossils are treated in the following pages.

If one were to single out three topics on which there has in recent years been a major shift of opinion, the first would be in the field of human palaeontology. Thanks to the magisterial lucidity of Sir Wilfrid Le Gros Clark's expositions and to the activities of a new and highly professional generation of physical anthropologists, the findings of this important branch of science are becoming much more intelligible than they were only a few years ago. Instead of a maze of idiosyncratic classifications designed to suit personal interpretations of exiguous fossils, we now have a much broader measure of professional agreement both as to classification and nomenclature and as to the most significant objectives for future research. There is, for instance, a broad consensus that the Genus *Homo* ought to be extended to comprise a substantially wider range of fossil forms, so that the so-called Pithecanthropines, including what were formerly classified as *Pithecanthropus* and *Sinanthropus*, are now generally referred to under the new designation *Homo erectus*. Again, a clearer light has been thrown on the several forms of *Australopithecus* and a new turn has been given to the discussion whether Australopithecines were or were not responsible for the stone tools with which they have occasionally been found through Dr Louis Leakey's discovery in Bed 1 at Olduvai of fossils of a type of hominid standing anatomically somewhere between *Australopithecus* and *Homo erectus*. Anthropologists are still divided on the question whether to regard these fossils as representative of a more advanced form of *Australopithecus* or whether to follow Professor Tobias and classify them as belonging to a new species of *Homo*, as *Homo habilis*. What seems common ground is that the newly recognized hominid made the tools with which his remains have been found.

Another important field in which there have been exceptionally important developments is that of Palaeolithic Cave Art. New discoveries in the west Mediterranean and in the Ural Mountains have notably extended the range of the art. Even more significant than new discoveries has been the re-evaluation of the familiar documents of Franco-Cantabric art, a re-evaluation which has gained in impetus from the passing of the great master and uncoverer of cave art, the Abbé Henri Breuil. Professor Leroi-Gourhan and his followers have prompted two important revisions. In the first place they have convinced most prehistorians that the Franco-Cantabric art passed through one and not two phases of development, and secondly they have initiated a new and more intensive phase of research into the meaning of the art. Instead of seeking to explain it first and foremost in terms of ethnographic comparisons, they have urged the necessity of concentrating study on the original documents, taking particular account of their positioning and associations as well as of their conventions. It is probably too soon to be sure of the validity of their conclusions, which are in any case only provisional, but already it seems plain that important new lines of investigation have been opened up. Again, it seems clear that earlier interpretations have leaned too heavily on hunting magic and paid too little attention to the symbolic character of the art and in particular to its sexual meaning.

A third topic on which I would like to comment is the transition from hunting and gathering to farming as the basic means of winning food. The contrast between the culture of what Lubbock was the first to distinguish over a hundred years ago as Palaeolithic and Neolithic man has remained a valid one, but recent work has re-emphasized the basic continuity of prehistory. In some ways Gordon Childe made his greatest contribution to the advance of prehistoric studies by highlighting through his phrase 'the Neolithic Revolution' the dynamic effect on the whole subsequent history of mankind of the adoption of farming. It was after all the stimulus of Childe's ideas that more than anything else led to a greater emphasis on exploring what underlay the beginnings of settled life in south-west Asia. As the results of excavations by Robert Braidwood, Kathleen Kenyon, James Mellaart, Ralph Solecki and others become more fully available they only serve to emphasize the revolutionary implications of farming. Yet as so often happens in research they have in an important respect undermined the validity of the basic concept. Powerfully aided by radio-carbon analysis they have underlined the fact that the transition from hunting and food-gathering to farming was one of extreme gradualness. What we see therefore is more a Transformation than a Revolution, a Transformation so gradual as only to be susceptible to close statistical analysis of the manner in which communities managed to render more abundant and secure their basis of subsistence. If we still need to stress the dichotomy between Palaeolithic and Neolithic, we also need to accept that prehistory was in fact continuous and recognize the role of the Transitional or Mesolithic communities in effecting the change from intensive hunting and gathering to incipient domestication of animals and plants. To strike a personal note, I also welcome the opportunity to lessen the emphasis which I have previously laid on climatic change as an agent in the process of economic and social change. I continue to think that the onset of Neothermal conditions had an inhibiting effect on the hunter-fisher inhabitants of north-western Europe, even if ultimately they made possible the infiltration of the new and more productive economy. In the decisive zone of south-west Asia on the other hand climatic change was clearly a matter of relatively minor importance except for marginal lands. The gradual transformation of the basis of subsistence was the outcome of a process beginning far back in the Pleistocene and one which in our own time has been given a new intensification as a result of modern knowledge of genetics and cybernetics. It has been by enlarging and making more certain his basis of subsistence that man has been able to live for longer life-spans in larger communities and at the same time to enjoy a richer cultural life.

In drawing on illustrations from ethnographic sources I do so with a more limited object than did W. J. Sollas in his *Ancient Hunters*, the last edition of which was issued in 1924. Since then we have given up the notion surviving from the old evolutionary era of Anthropology that existing peoples can be interpreted as outcrops of earlier layers of human prehistory and can so be used to fill gaps and explain archaeological data. We recognize that the aborigines of central and northern Australia or the Bushmen of the Kalahari live on the same plane of time as we do and practice cultures as unique as our own. What we can legitimately do is to recognize that such peoples as the Australian aborigines and the Bushmen were limited by the same kind of factors as restricted the opportunities open to our Palaeolithic and Mesolithic forebears. With the almost unlimited horizons open to us in our age of science and metropolitan living, we need the help they can give us in trying to imagine the kind of life lived by our remote forebears.

G. C.

CHAPTER ONE

Man as Primate

A fundamental attraction of archaeology is that it tells us not merely about the material fabric of our civilization and its history from primitive beginnings but about ourselves and our very humanity. If we review the course of human history we can recognize certain crucial thresholds, the crossing of which have led us to progressively fuller possibilities of life. Among the more prominent of these are the invention and adoption of farming, the achievement of literacy and city life, and in recent times the industrial and scientific revolutions. Yet, important as these are, none of them can begin to compare in importance with the process of attaining humanity, a process that must have taken an immensely long time and about which we still know remarkably little.

The essential predicament of man is that he is aware of his situation as an animal but is yet potentially divine. If through the power of his imagination he is capable of comprehending the workings of the cosmos, penetrating the mystery of life and reconstructing his own past, he has to eat and reproduce like any beast of the field and like them he has to die. Even the apparent dichotomy between body and soul can only be appreciated by what is itself a physical organ, the brain, the seat of man's powers of thought, discrimination and self-awareness, the powers on which his specifically human character depends. As an organism man has emerged comparatively recently in the course of biological evolution, a process which, so far as this planet is concerned, began some two thousand million years ago with the first appearance of organic life.

Zoological Classification

If we accept that man in fact developed by a gradual evolution from earlier forms of life, it follows that we can hardly expect to be able to point to any narrowly defined date by which he may be said to have first appeared on the scene. Again, although several new scientific methods are available for dating the deposits containing traces of the earliest men and their culture, much uncertainty still remains about early dates. At present it can only be said that the Pleistocene period, to which all human fossils belong, probably began about two million years ago.

The following classification shows the position of the Genus *Homo* in relation to the most closely related members of the Order *Primates*:

Sub-orders	Super-families	Families	Genera
PROSIMII			
ANTHROPOIDEA	{ *Ceboidea* *Cercopithecoidea* *Hominoidea*	{ *Pongidae* *Hominidae*	{ *Australopithecus* *Homo*

Zoologically speaking, all kinds of men, living and fossil, belong to the hominid family (*Hominidae*) which, together with the great apes and gibbons (*Pongidae*) form the hominoids (*Hominoidea*), one of three super-families of the sub-order *Anthropoidea* of the order *Primates*. The hominids appear to have diverged from the pongids during a period of increasingly arid conditions in the Miocene period. During this time of marked ecological change between thirty and fifteen million years ago, when grasslands expanded greatly at the expense of forest, the anthropoid forebears of the surviving great apes maintained their hold on the diminishing forest tracts, whereas others, prototypes of the hominids, took to a more open life in the savannah. It is interesting to reflect that those anthropoids who by their superior strength were able to defend their hold on a familiar habitat only survive, whether as inmates of zoos or as protected fauna in the wild, by grace of man, the descendant of those compelled by relative weakness to adapt to new conditions. This is a story sufficiently familiar in the history of biological evolution, but its relevance is still not always appreciated in our own day and in our own society.

If it is true that man has emerged like other organisms in the process of biological evolution, the question arises how far we can learn about his behaviour from a study of animals. Men after all are still organisms, even men of the most advanced civilizations, and as such their lives are still regulated and patterned by basic biological facts. All human cultures – and here one includes social structure and systems of belief as much as technology and practical knowledge – subserve the basic aim of life, which is quite simply to survive. Cultural forms which stand in the way of this either change or else disappear from the historical record as surely as organisms that fail to adapt to their environment disappear from the biological world. This is why archaeology discloses by and large a story of progress. Of course individual societies and particular patterns of culture have failed to make effective adjustments, but since these disappear they cease to leave fossils behind them: the archaeological record by its very nature preserves the history of those communities that have succeeded in surviving up to the time represented by the structures or other artifacts dug up by the archaeologist. Biologically the success of man has indeed been overwhelming. To take only one measure of fitness in natural selection, there is the evidence of his increase in numbers. This may be seen in the following table giving the estimated population of the world, in millions, at widely separated periods of time:

A D 2000 (U.N. estimate)	6267
1967	3000
1650	500/550
Roman Empire	150/200
Middle Palaeolithic	1

It follows that by and large human culture must have been adaptive: it has favoured the biological success of man and in doing so it has necessarily undergone a continuous process of change. The fossil records of this process is what archaeologists primarily study. Man has survived like any other organism by eating and reproducing; but he has attained his dominant position through the medium of his transmitted and constantly increasing heritage of culture.

Human and Animal Behaviour

The possibility has to be considered that something could be learned about human behaviour by studying that of the non-human primates. There is certainly a better chance of gaining insights of value now that studies are being made of apes and monkeys living in their natural habitats instead of concentrating on the frustrated denizens of zoos. Even so, we do well to remember that though the great apes may be man's closest surviving relative they are still extremely remote. The immediate predecessors of man survive only in the form of fragmentary fossils. In so far as living apes and monkeys do help our understanding of behaviour it is very largely by pointing contrasts. A few of these only need be mentioned.

1 Gorillas aloft in forest trees. The photograph shows, *upper left*, a female nursing an infant, *lower middle*, a young male and, *lower right*, a female beating her breast. It should be emphasized that adult males in particular spend most of their time on the ground and, on occasion, even adopt an upright stance

By contrast with man, capable of adapting to a wide range of natural conditions, the non-human primates are normally restricted to comparatively specialized habitats. Within their living areas most primates tend to observe more or less strict territorial boundaries, but whereas among apes relations between groups are either exclusive or, as with the Mountain Gorilla, passive, in mankind active and for the most part friendly interrelations exist. In daily life tools, so important in human society, play only a subsidiary role among apes. Again, constructions are limited as a rule to nests on the ground or crude platforms in trees and these never form permanent or

Ill. 1

17

even durable homes. Communication among the non-human primates is at an extremely simple level by contrast with even the most elementary human language. Vital differences appear also in the spheres most directly relevant to survival, namely food and sex. Whereas among apes and monkeys there is no sharing of food between individuals over the age of infancy, human society is to an important extent based precisely on this. Again, sexual relationships in human society are subject to cultural regulation instead of resting on the shifting basis of male domination. Behaviour of a distinctively human order rests on artificial conventions, conventions that differ from one group to another. Again, in all the most vital areas human societies outside the range of modern political systems are unique in being regulated and sustained by a complex web of kinship obligations.

Fossil Hominids

If something can be learned from a study of surviving hunter-fishers (see chapter 6), the fact remains that the behaviour of representatives of earlier forms of hominid cannot be studied directly for the simple reason that they have long been extinct. Our knowledge of *Australopithecus* or of *Homo erectus* is restricted to what can be learned from their physical traces and from material manifestations of their culture; and it remains true, as Sir Wilfrid Le Gros Clark pointed out in 1955, that neither hominid fossils nor artificially shaped tools have yet been found in deposits anterior to the Early Pleistocene, a period now thought to have lasted longer than the Middle and Late Pleistocene by a factor of three or four and to have begun about two million years ago.

Some of the leading characteristics of man and his more recent forebears were already acquired while they lived to a large extent in the trees. It was for instance during this phase that the limbs developed their powers of prehension

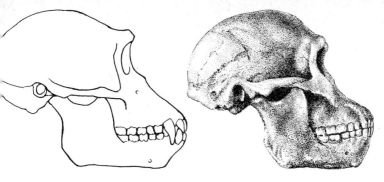

2 The skull of a chimpanzee, *left*, compared to the skull of *Australopithecus transvaalensis*, *right*. The former is enlarged to assist the comparison

and that sight gained so markedly on smell as the leading organ of sensory perception. On the other hand it was on the ground that habitual upright posture and bi-pedal stance were adopted, freeing the hands for tool-using and ultimately for tool-making. The importance of this step led physical anthropologists a few years ago to concentrate attention on the Australopithecines, lightly built and small-brained but upright-standing hominids, fossils of whom have come to light in increasing numbers in South and East Africa, as possible makers of the earliest stone industries. *Australopithecus*, which forms a genus of the *Hominidae* distinct from the various species of *Homo*, existed in at least three main groups. Of these *A. boisei* (once given generic status by Dr Leakey as *Zinjanthropus*) occurred already in Bed I of the sequence of Pleistocene deposits exposed in the gorge of Olduvai in Tanzania. Another Early Pleistocene form is *A. africanus*, represented by finds from Makapansgat, Sterkfontein and Taungs, a form marked among other features by notably smaller teeth. A third species *A. robustus* (*cf. Paranthropus*) is represented by fossils from Middle Pleistocene deposits at Kromdrai and Swartkrans as well as from Tanzania.

Ill. 2

Ill. 3

The question arises how far if at all the Australopithecines made stone tools. The first point to emphasise is that the great majority of Australopithecine fossils came from deposits without any trace of stone implements. The second is that when tools are found in the same layers as remains of Australopithecines these are usually accompanied

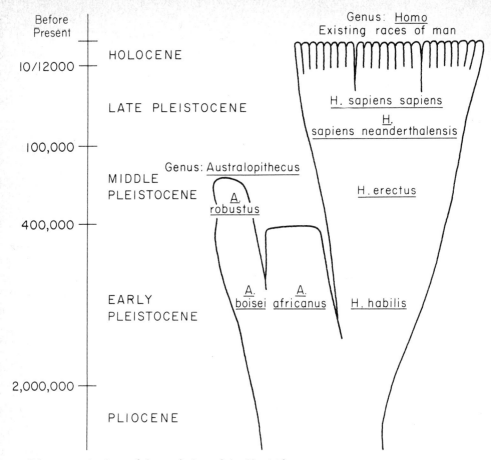

Before
Present

10/12000

100,000

400,000

2,000,000

HOLOCENE

LATE PLEISTOCENE

MIDDLE
PLEISTOCENE

EARLY
PLEISTOCENE

PLIOCENE

Genus: Homo
Existing races of man

H. sapiens sapiens

H.
sapiens neanderthalensis

Genus: Australopithecus

A.
robustus

H. erectus

A.   A.
boisei africanus

H. habilis

3 Diagrammatic chart of the evolution of the *Hominidae*

by the bones of other more advanced types of hominid; in such cases the suggestion is that *Australopithecus* was himself a victim of the tool-makers. Suspicions that some other hominid more directly in line with human development may have been responsible for Early Pleistocene stone implements have recently been strongly confirmed as a result of detailed study of skull and jaw-bones and teeth recovered by Dr and Mrs Leakey from Bed I at Olduvai. Indeed these fossils, fragmentary though they are, are now recognized to belong to a type of hominid more advanced than previously known Australopithecines. Some anthropologists believe that these still fall within the range of variation of *Australopithecus africanus*, but Dr Tobias and Dr Napier prefer to classify them within the genus *Homo*, as *Homo habilis*. The new form is distinguished by having smaller teeth and a larger brain than the Australopithecines. Furthermore, it is particularly interesting that study of the hand-bones of *Homo habilis* suggests that he had the ability to exert a true power grip, fully adequate to shape pebble choppers, even if he still lacked the precision needed to make finer tools.

The Growth of the Brain

After an upright stance had been attained, the next main line of anatomical change lay in increases in the size of the brain, increases which helped to make possible, but at the same time were stimulated by increased manual dexterity and the manufacture and manipulation of increasingly effective tools. The fragmentary nature of many fossil skulls means that it is often only possible to estimate very approximately the capacity of the brains they once enclosed and, again, the numbers of specimens available is as a rule too small to provide an adequate sample for each category. Nevertheless, if estimates for brain capacity are plotted the overall picture is sufficiently plain. The position may be highlighted by pointing out that the maximum size of modern man's brain is nearly treble that of even the largest-brained Australopithecine and nearly twice as much as that of *Homo erectus* from Trinil, Java.

Ill. 4

The table brings out another point of great importance, namely that the increase in the size of the brain is progressive. This fits in very well with the modern way of viewing hominid evolution. The idea, still enshrined in some textbooks, that most hominid fossils represent extinct forms that diverged from the stem of an evolutionary tree crowned by modern man is now largely replaced by

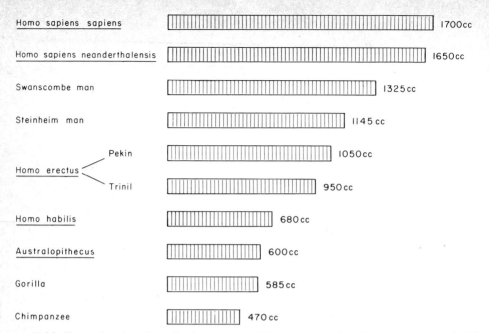

Homo sapiens sapiens		1700cc
Homo sapiens neanderthalensis		1650cc
Swanscombe man		1325cc
Steinheim man		1145cc
Homo erectus — Pekin		1050cc
Homo erectus — Trinil		950cc
Homo habilis		680cc
Australopithecus		600cc
Gorilla		585cc
Chimpanzee		470cc

4   Table illustrating the relative brain capacity of chimpanzees and modern man compared with those of fossil men

the notion of broad evolutionary stages or steps. This in turn is reflected in the new nomenclature. Instead of relegating the early Middle Pleistocene fossils from Trinil (Java) and from Choukoutien (China) to a special genus, *Pithecanthropus*, Sir Wilfrid Le Gros Clark and his pupils prefer to include both within the Genus *Homo* under the species name *Homo erectus*; indeed, as we have seen, even the Early Pleistocene fossil, once known as *Zinjanthropus*, is now included in the genus as *Homo habilis*. In the same way, Neanderthal man is no longer thought of as standing mainly or even wholly to one side as a kind of poor cousin of *Homo sapiens*, but rather as a sub-specific variant of the same species: if some varieties of Neanderthal man are still considered to have diverged from the main line, others are held to stand as representatives of an important phase of hominid evolution. Into such a picture of evolutionary development fossils like those from Swanscombe or Steinheim fall quite easily

Ill. 5

5 The fragments of the Swanscombe Skull found in the Barnfield gravel pit at Swanscombe, Kent. They were found over a period of some thirty years

into their distinctive niches between *Homo erectus* and *Homo sapiens neanderthalensis*.

Tools and Speech

Although physical anthropologists normally define man as a species in terms of certain anatomical characteristics, most of us think in terms of his behaviour; we recognize that an upright stance, hands capable of skilled manipulation, and a powerful brain, were necessary prerequisites, but we are rightly more directly concerned with the fact of culture than with the biological attributes that made this possible on a human scale. One of man's most notable characteristics is his ability to make and use tools and it is fortunate that from an early stage he made these among other things from highly imperishable materials like flint and stone. Of course many other primates than man make use of extraneous materials to supplement their own limbs in furthering their aims. When observed in captivity, for example, apes show considerable ingenuity in manipulating sticks and strings or in stacking boxes, and in the wild state they have been seen to shape branches and stalks to assist them in acquiring tasty but otherwise inaccessible food. Yet always, when using or even fabricating tools, the great apes direct their energies to securing immediately visible objectives. Again, their use and preparation of tools is based rather on improvization and imitation than on patterns transmitted through cultural traditions.

Culture, in the sense of modes of behaviour learned rather than inherited by inborn instinct, is certainly no monopoly of man. It has been shown for example that patterns of bird song may vary locally within a single species, pointing to learning against mere heredity. Yet, if culture cannot in all senses of the term be held as exclusive to man, there can be no question that in the course of prehistory it was developed among men to a degree never approached among the non-human primates. Moreover, in human society tools were made not merely to achieve immediately perceived aims but rather to meet future contingencies; stone tools for instance were designed to make implements, weapons or ornaments from organic materials. Again the tools made by man generally involved a much greater modification of natural substances than was the case among the non-human primates, and these modifications were made in accordance with styles prevailing in particular societies.

The development of technology is only one aspect of cultural behaviour, albeit one that happens to survive best in the archaeological record, yet it does illustrate in its history another feature of human culture, namely its progressive, accumulative character. This in turn must have depended on a mechanism of transmission superior to what was available to other animals. Imitation was doubtless an important mechanism for transmitting cultural behaviour from one generation to another, more particularly in the sphere of technology, yet there is no doubt that one of man's greatest advantages in this respect has been his capacity for communicating by means of symbols. There seems to be general agreement that one of the biggest drawbacks suffered by the great apes in comparison with even the simplest human communities is their limited range of communication. It is true that chimpanzees have a very wide 'register of emotional expression' and that they are able to communicate not only their emotional states but also definite desires; yet, as Kohler has emphasized, 'their gamut of phonetics is entirely subjective and can only express emotions, never designate or describe objects'. In their heroic enterprise of rearing the chimpanzee Vicky from the age of three days to three years, Dr and Mrs Hayes found it possible to train her to commands, but failed after eighteen months of intensive tuition to get her to identify her nose, hands, eyes or feet. Until men had learned to employ words as symbols and communicate by means of articulate speech their capacity to transmit and so accumulate any considerable body of culture was severely limited. By the nature of things it is hardly possible to measure progress in the development of language before written records become available. On the other hand it may well be that the exceedingly slow rate of cultural advance throughout the Early and Middle Pleistocene was due to the rudimentary nature of language during this time; and, conversely, the sudden acceleration of cultural development during the latter half of the Upper Pleistocene within a comparatively limited zone of the Old World may well reflect a breakthrough on the linguistic front.

CHAPTER TWO

Early Hunters

Stone Work of the Lower Pleistocene

It is not easy to detect the earliest essays in making flint
and stone tools. The transition from using whatever lay
at hand to fashioning tools was gradual and ill-defined;
natural fragments of flint or stone might for example be
adapted for use with only the minimum of artificial
shaping. There is also the special difficulty that natural
and artificial flints unfortunately often resemble each
other and in the past mistakes have been made. Flints that
used to be thought examples of early workmanship are
now known to occur in certain types of natural deposit of
widely varying geological age and in some cases it is even
possible to observe them at the present day in process of
formation. The earliest well dated stone industries which
can be certainly recognized are those from Lower
Pleistocene deposits like those at Olduvai Gorge in
Tanzania, which yielded traces of *Homo habilis*.

It seems that, at any rate during the season represented
by the living floors which exist at different levels of
Bed I at Olduvai, the early men were occupying mud
flats near the lake then present in the gorge. The debris
consisted of natural stones that must have been brought
to the site: stones showing signs of having been used for
bashing; primitive stone tools, together with the waste

Ill. 6

6 Olduvai Gorge in Tanzania is over 300 feet deep. In the steep walls of the gorge traces of successive periods of human occupation have been found going back to Lower Pleistocene times

material resulting from their manufacture, and animal bones, nearly every one of which that could have contained marrow having been broken in small fragments. The treatment of the animal bones and the close association of these with stone implements and bashers shows the importance of meat and bone marrow in the diet. Clearly these early men, in marked contrast with the surviving great apes, who live to a large extent though not exclusively on plant food, were already hunters, even if, as Dr Leakey claims, they concentrated on small game, including birds, fish and reptiles, eked out perhaps by scavenging the prey of larger mammals. The most important element in the tool kit was the generalized chopping tool made by striking off a few flakes from a stone pebble, sometimes from one face only but in the case of thicker ones, often from both. Stone industries of a similar kind have long been known from early deposits in North Africa, particularly from Algeria and Morocco and very recently have been recovered even farther north from a late Early Pleistocene deposit near Vértesszöllös in western Hungary.

Ill. 7

27

It is too soon to know whether or not East Africa will prove to have been the original focus of the most primitive stone industries. Very possibly the development took place over extensive areas, individual advances in technique being made at different centres over wide territories. Pebble and flake industries of Oldowan type from Lower Pleistocene deposits in Morocco appear in their earliest phase to be more primitive than those found in Bed I at Olduvai and may even be earlier in age. Recent investigations at Kota Tampan in an apparently Early Pleistocene terrace of the Perak River in northern Malaya have revealed a stone industry of the same general type, suggesting that South-East Asia may have fallen within the original province of the pebble and flake culture, or at least that this culture had spread there earlier than had previously been thought.

Big Game Hunters of the Middle Pleistocene

The Middle Pleistocene witnessed a notable advance in the physical evolution of man in the appearance of *Homo erectus*, a hominid with a markedly larger brain and one which, as we have seen, was formerly grouped within the distinct species *Pithecanthropus* and popularly referred to as Pithecanthropine. In the Olduvai Gorge itself and at Ternifine in Algeria remains of *Homo erectus* have been found with traces of a new tradition of flint and stone working characterized above all by the production of bifacial hand-axes, which were almost certainly an African invention. On the other hand some of the most important finds of *Homo erectus* have been made in Java

Ill. 8

and in China at Chenchiawo in Shensi, and at Choukoutien near Peking, associated with pebble and flake industries of the old tradition.

The best documented discoveries of Middle Pleistocene date in the Far East are beyond question those made in the rock fissures at Choukoutien. The finds made in these

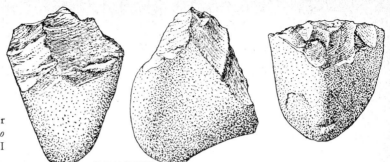

7 Pebble chopper tools used by *Homo habilis* from Bed I at Olduvai Gorge

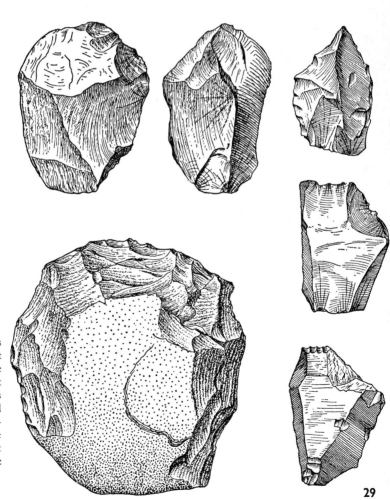

8 Implements from Locality I at Choukoutien. The tools on the left are chopping tools of quartz and greenstone respectively. The three tools on the right are flakes of quartz

Maurice Wilson 1950

Ills. 9, 10

leave no doubt that Peking man was a heavy meat-eater: bones of many animals were present, those represented including deer, antelope, horse, wild pig, bison, water-buffalo, elephant, rhinoceros and monkey, as well as several species of carnivore. The association of these with ash deposits indicative of fireplaces, the way the bones were broken for marrow and the presence of a variety of scratches and cut-marks all make it clear that in the main at any rate these bones represent traces of animals eaten for food, and their abundance can only mean that they were hunted. Signs of the use of fire are among the earliest known, though one can hardly tell whether the fire was intended mainly for cooking, protection, warmth

Ill. 11

or in the hunting of driven game. It is well to ask how *Homo erectus* was able to gain a mastery over so wide a range of animals, many of them fleeter and stronger than himself? The answer is twofold, by his brain and by his culture. The only weapons certainly attributable to Lower

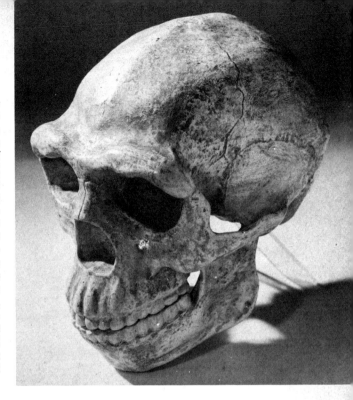

9, 10 Peking man, *Homo erectus pekinensis*, was a meat-eater and to judge from damage at the base of skulls he also seems to have extracted the brains of his fellows, perhaps for ritual eating (*cf. ills. 20, 21*). His brain capacity was larger than that of his predecessors (*see ill. 4*) and this must have given him an advantage in coping with his environment and hunting successfully a variety of large animals. He also knew the use of fire. The reconstruction of a cave at Choukoutien, *left*, closely follows the archaeological evidence of finds at the site and the reconstructed skull, *right*, is based on an almost complete example found there

Palaeolithic man are wooden spears with tips pointed and hardened in the fire like those found in interglacial deposits at Clacton, Essex, and Lohringen, Lower Saxony. His technical means were elementary indeed. The tools he made from quartz, greenstone and coarse chert are so crude in appearance that many of them would hardly be recognizable as such had they not been found in and around his fireplaces mixed with discarded meat bones. Among them may be listed rough flakes, some with 'bipolar' scars caused by crushing between two boulders, and crude chopper tools made by striking flakes in either direction from the edge of a flake or pebble. There are signs that antler and animal bones were utilized and even on occasion cut into sections for convenience, but there is no evidence that these materials were used for making carefully formed implements. Indeed there is no sign among his surviving equipment of any specific hunting weapon and it is safe to assume that he relied on wooden

Ill. 12

Ill. 8

11 Australian aborigines setting light to the bush in order to drive game in the direction of waiting hunters

13 The Lower Palaeolithic world with some of the more notable sites where remains have been found

spears shaped by stone tools and hardened in the fire. Fire may also have been used to stampede or head off game and in conjunction with this the concerted operations of even quite a small band of hunters may well have been sufficient to drive animals over steep places and so disable them. Pit-traps may have been used to catch or at least maim large game and young animals could have been run down on foot. What is certain is that in Middle Pleistocene China *Homo erectus*, with a tool-kit little if any superior to what had earlier been available in Africa, managed to secure even large game animals in considerable variety. Beyond question it was as hunters that the earliest men found themselves and achieved their new status in the biological world.

Before returning to Africa to take stock of new developments it is worth noting that pebble and flake industries in a broad sense similar to those from Chou-koutien, though displaying regional features, existed

12 Tip of a wooden spearhead of Middle Palaeolithic date from Clacton, Essex

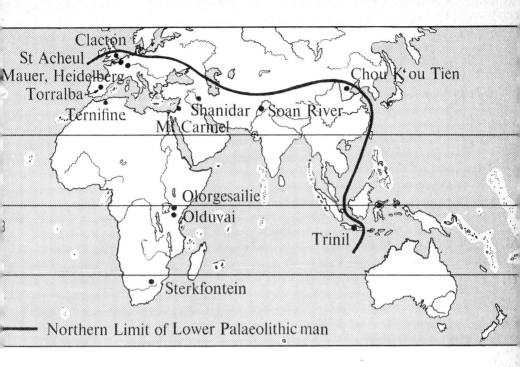

Clacton
St Acheul
Mauer, Heidelberg
Torralba
Ternifine
Shanidar Soan River
Mt Carmel
Chou K'ou Tien

Olorgesailie
Olduvai
Trinil

Sterkfontein

—— Northern Limit of Lower Palaeolithic man

Ill. 13

during the Middle Pleistocene in different parts of the
Eurasiatic land-mass from the Clactonian of south-
eastern England and parts of north-western Europe to
the Soan of the Punjab, the Anyathian of Burma and the
Pajitanian of Java. Indeed the pebble and flake tradition
seems to have persisted throughout the Pleistocene in
some parts of South-East Asia and was even carried to
Australia before the end of the Ice Age.

The most significant development of the Middle
Pleistocene was without doubt the emergence of the
hand-axe or *coup de poing*. This was made by thinning down
a nodule or thick flake on two faces to form an edge that
was usually confined to one end but might in highly
evolved specimens run all the way round. The assumption
is that hand-axes were probably grasped directly in the
hand, the most versatile and accommodating of holders,
and used for such purposes as grubbing up roots, cutting
up game and even shaping wood. They were made from

Ill. 16

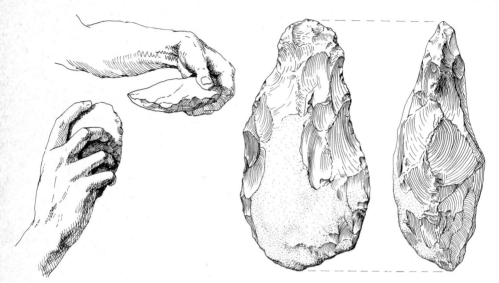

14 Hand-axes of flint or stone, like this one of Abbevillian type, were made from nodules or thick flakes by repeated blows directed from the edge in either direction. The tool could always be resharpened if need be by the same method

a wide range of raw materials, from flint and obsidian to the more difficult quartzes, quartzites, lavas and even granites; yet the degree of standardization is often remarkable. There is no doubt that Africa was the cradle of the hand-axe industries. One reason for thinking so is the geographical distribution of this easily-recognizable tool, which is found over the whole of Africa, excluding only the equatorial rain-forest and parts of the Horn, and in near-by parts of Western Europe and South-East Asia. The only apparent isolated area is peninsular India, but it has to be remembered that sea-levels were much lower at times of maximum glaciation and sites with hand-axes may well have existed on the bed of what is now the Persian Gulf and on submerged surfaces off the south coast of the Iranian plateau.

Hand-axes were leading tools over immense periods of time within much of this territory. When one examines a series from successive levels of a stratified site such as

15, 16   The Acheulean hand-axe, *left*, seen in front view and profile, was an all-purpose tool, slim enough to fit easily into the hand as can be seen in the detail, *right*, of an aborigine holding a similar type of hand-axe

Olduvai it is possible to see broad evolutionary trends. Pointed pebble tools from the base of Bed II provide satisfactory prototypes for the earliest true hand-axes found in the upper part of that Bed, and which are comparable in relative thickness and irregularity of working edge with those of the Abbevillian phase of French prehistory. Progressively improved skill enabled the palaeolithic workers to turn out shapelier hand-axes from smaller quantities of flint or stone, hand-axes of a kind commonly referred to as Acheulean after the French site of St Acheul. Of course not all hand-axes from the later periods were more shapely than those from earlier ones; one can only say there was some advance in the finest specimens. It would almost certainly be wrong to accept this as the result of a conscious desire for efficiency; much more likely was it the outcome of the feeling for craftsmanship, even for aesthetic gratification, stimulated perhaps by a drive for social emulation. Hand-axes were

Ill. 14

Ill. 15

only one of several kinds of tool. In early levels both in East and North Africa they were normally accompanied by pebble and flake tools of the old style and during the later phases (often referred to as Acheulean) they formed part of quite an extensive tool-kit, including cleavers having a broad cutting edge rather than a point, heavy picks and spheroids, steep core-scrapers and other implements made from fine small flakes. Wooden objects are naturally only rarely found from this period, but there is no doubt that they played an important part in the equipment of Acheulean man, notably as spears, digging-sticks and clubs. On the other hand there is no evidence that man had yet begun to mount his flint implements on wooden handles or hafts.

Indications from Africa are that Acheulean culture was adapted to the savannah. Camping-places were normally set within easy reach of water. For example, at Olorgesaile in Kenya, Acheulean man lived like his forebears of Bed I at Olduvai on alluvial flats surrounding a lake. The banks of the lake itself seem to have been avoided, possibly on account of mosquitoes or in order to avoid disturbing game. The locations chosen for actual occupation were commonly sandy patches along the courses of seasonal runnels; these would have been free of vegetation and no doubt water could have been secured from them by scooping into the bed. Investigation of patches of worked flint and animal bone at Olorgesaile have shown that these fall as a rule into two main sizes, very small ones only five or six metres across, and larger ones some fifteen or sixteen metres in diameter. The fact that the beds of water-courses were often chosen for occupation under-lines the impermanence of settlement and it may be that the size of the social group, which can never have amounted to more than a very small number of adults, may have varied at different times of the year. The areas of occupation at Olorgesaile were sharply defined as if to suggest that they were limited by some form of shelter or possibly even by a thorn-bush hedge. There are also signs in the final Acheulean level (55650 BC ±50) of the Kalambo Falls site at the southern end of Lake Tanganyika of a curved setting of stone boulders marking perhaps the site of an elementary fish-weir or, alternatively, the base of an artificial wind-break. The fact that the first unequivocal evidence for the use of fire in Africa occurs at this time suggest that this important discovery may have spread there from Asia, where, as we have seen at Choukoutien, it was a common possession already well back in the Middle Pleistocene.

Ill. 9

An interesting result of exploring settlement sites is the light it throws on the food eaten by the hand-axe people. Organic traces from the living floors at Kalambo Falls show that fruits, seeds and nuts contributed to the diet of Acheulean man. On the other hand the hand-axe makers, like the men of Choukoutein, were above all hunters and meat-eaters: at Torralba in Spain they accounted for elephant and rhinoceros as well as for smaller quarry like ox, stag and horse, and at Olorgesaile they killed and smashed open the skulls of hippopotami and of giant kinds of horse, pig, sheep and baboon.

Culture of Neanderthal Man

Prehistorians no longer believe in the separate existence of flake and core-tool traditions in Africa and its extensions: flake tools were present even in the Oldowayan, were a leading element of the Clactonian variant and played a definite role even in the predominantly hand-axe industries of Acheulean type. On the other hand there is evidence that for whatever reason the relative importance of the hand-axe and flake components underwent a definite change around the time of transition from Middle to Upper Pleistocene and that this took place earlier and more pronouncedly in the northern part of the province,

17, 18 *Left.* Thin flakes of predetermined form could be struck from tortoise-shaped cores prepared by radial flaking. This technique is called after the French locality of Levallois. *Above* are examples of tools made by Neanderthal man, a point, bone anvil and side-scraper from La Quina

Ill. 18
Ill. 17

notably in southern Europe, North Africa and southwest Asia. Several distinct industrial traditions appeared at this time in the northern part of the Palaeolithic world. One, named after Levallois near Paris, is marked by their preparation of cores resembling tortoises in the general form. The idea was to shape the block of flint stone in such a way that flakes could be struck from one face ready to use as they came, or at most needing only slight modification; as a result of this preparation the butts of Levallois flakes were usually faceted. Another tradition of flint-work, that first identified at the cave of Le Moustier, involved the striking of flakes from disc-cores and the conversion of some of these into side-scrapers or points by means of a particular kind of step flaking. The makers of such Mousterian industries continued to make hand-axes, including cordiform and triangular shapes, over much of Western Europe. In Eastern Europe, on the other hand, from the Rhine to the Volga, in the Greek and

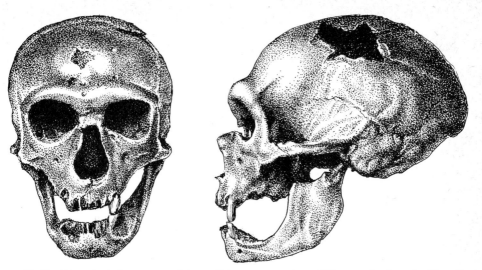

19 Skull of Neanderthal man, one of the earliest representatives of *Homo sapiens* from La Chapelle-aux-Saints. His brain capacity approaches that of Modern man (*cf. ill. 4*)

Italian peninsulas, and on the French riviera, they made no hand-axes or at least very few, but converted flakes into a number of special forms including numerous awls, fusiform pieces with plano-convex touch and narrow strip flakes with abrupt retouch down one edge. Lastly there were parts of North Africa and south-west Asia, including notably Palestine, where we find assemblages most conveniently described as Levalloiso-Mousterian.

The makers of these industries, referred to by some prehistorians as Middle Palaeolithic, belonged to a physically more evolved type, having in some cases a brain as large as that of modern man. Some kinds of Neanderthal man, named after the original fossil from the locality of that name in the Rhineland, were far from prepossessing in appearance. One of the first things one would have noticed about them would have been their slouching carriage, their protruding brow-ridges, and receding foreheads. Indeed it was usual at one time to treat

Ill. 19

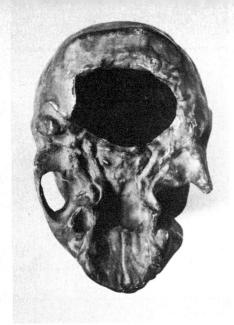

20, 21   Two skulls showing damage to the *foramen magnum* made in the course of extracting the brain for ritual or cannibal purposes. The example *left* is of Neanderthal type and was found in a ritual context in a cave at Monte Circeo, south of Rome. *Right* is the skull of a modern Melanesian cannibal showing the same kind of damage

Ill. 4

Neanderthal man as if he belonged to a distinct species (*Homo neanderthalensis*), a side branch that diverged from the evolutionary tree. On the other hand, the size of his brain has helped to persuade modern anthropologists that he belongs firmly in the category of *Homo sapiens*. The aberrant character of the West European group, cut off and isolated by the advance of the Alpine and Scandinavian ice-sheets, is admitted, but there is no difficulty in accepting many of the Neanderthal fossils from Italy and South Germany, as well as from Eastern Europe, North Africa and south-west Asia, as marking an evolutionary stage between *Homo erectus* and modern man (*Homo sapiens sapiens*). If this is so, it becomes very much easier to explain some very notable advances achieved at this time in the general progress of humanity. For one thing the frontiers of human settlement were pushed northwards at a time when glaciers were extending in northern and central Europe and in the mountain systems of Central

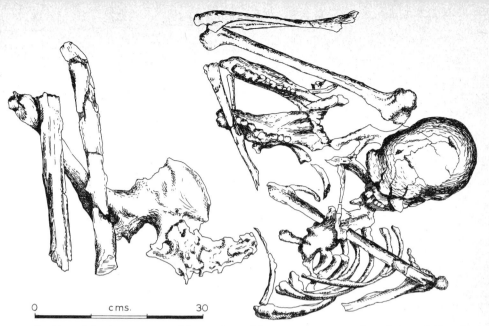

0 cms. 30

22 An idea of death as a personal fate and possibly some awareness of a religious feeling first appears in Neanderthal times. The careful burial of ten individuals in a cemetery on the terrace of Mugharet-es-Skhūl, Mont Carmel, shows this. Associated with one adult male burial from this site were the jawbones of a great wild boar which the skeleton is apparently clasping

Asia, an advance made possible by the possession of fire and the use of skin clothing, and one which brought much of Central Germany, southern Poland, the South Russian Plain, Iran, Turkmenia and even Uzbekistan within the range of human settlement.

But Neanderthal man advanced in a psychic as well as in a merely physical sense. Peking man, by breaking into the skulls of his dead in order to extract their brains, was probably doing more than satisfying a physical appetite; by analogy with recent Melanesian practice he was engaging in ritual cannibalism. On the other hand it was apparently Neanderthal man who initiated the practice of careful burial of the dead. On the terrace in front of the Mugharet-es-Skhūl, Mount Carmel, a regular cemetery of Neanderthal people was uncovered, comprising ten individuals, one of whom had a wound in one of his thigh bones, apparently made by a wooden spear. The Mount Carmel burials had their legs drawn up to the

Ills. 20, 21

Ill. 22

41

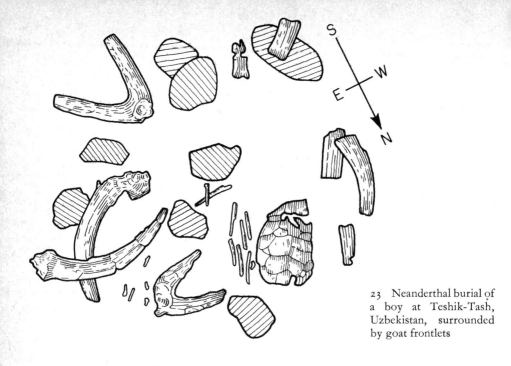

S
W
E
N

23 Neanderthal burial of a boy at Teshik-Tash, Uzbekistan, surrounded by goat frontlets

body, a practice also found in the case of the Neanderthal burial at Kiik-Koba, in the Crimea. No attempt seems to have been made at Mount Carmel to do more than place the dead in shallow graves, but the head of the man buried at La Ferrassie in France together with a woman and two children was apparently protected by stones. The woman, whose arms were folded, had her legs so tightly flexed as to suggest that the corpse may have been bound with thongs, a practice which may reflect a desire on the part of the living to keep the dead securely away. Among the few grave-goods found with a Neanderthal burial were the jaws of a great wild boar clasped in the arms of an adult male; personal ornaments were conspicuously absent. An unexplained ritual feature is that the burial of a Neanderthal boy at Teshik-Tash in Uzbekistan was apparently surrounded by goat frontlets having their horn-cores rammed into the soil.

Ill. 22

Ill. 23

CHAPTER THREE

Advanced Hunters

The latter half of the Upper Pleistocene beginning around
40,000 years ago witnessed developments of prime
importance to the future history of mankind. It saw in the
first place the final emergence of modern man (*Homo
sapiens sapiens*), his expansion over almost the whole earth
and the differentiation of many of the existing races of
man. As already noted Neanderthal man and his cousins
at a comparable level of evolutionary development in
southern Africa (Rhodesian man) and Indonesia (Solo
man), had large enough brains to qualify as *Homo sapiens*.
It is not in the size of his brain that modern man differs
from Neanderthal man but rather in his more upright
stance, his lighter jaw with more pointed chin and smaller
teeth and his less prominent brow-ridges, which no longer
form the continuous torus characteristic of Neanderthal
man.

Ills. 4, 24

Geographically the Late Pleistocene was marked,
particularly in its closing stages, by a great expansion in
the area of human settlement. As already noted, man of
the Neanderthal type had already broken out of the
comparatively narrow limits to which the earliest men
had been confined down to the earlier part of the Late
Pleistocene. The process now seems to have been carried
very much further and radio-carbon dates show that both

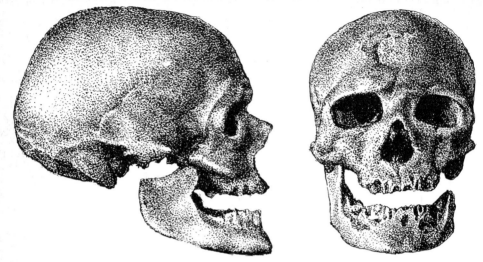

24 Skull of 'modern man', *Homo sapiens*, from Cro-Magnon, Dordogne. It is this type which is associated with the cave art of south-west France and northern Spain

the New World and Australasia were occupied well before the end of the Ice Age (10–12,000 years ago). Although certain anthropologists have argued that some of the main racial types of modern man, including the Australians, are of high antiquity and stem from an earlier phase in human evolution, the general view is that all surviving peoples belong alike to *Homo sapiens sapiens*. At all stages in their evolution there must have been a tendency to speciate in response to differing ecological circumstances and modern man was no exception to the general rule. Indeed since many of the physical characteristics used to distinguish racial varieties, such as pigmentation, hair form and breadth of nose, can plausibly be related to differences in climate, it seems reasonable to imagine that the movement into the more extreme environments may even have stimulated this process. It is interesting to reflect that the world as a whole was colonized by man while still a hunter and food-gatherer, even though he did not occupy some Arctic territories until well into Neothermal times. None of the territories which had to

Ill. 25

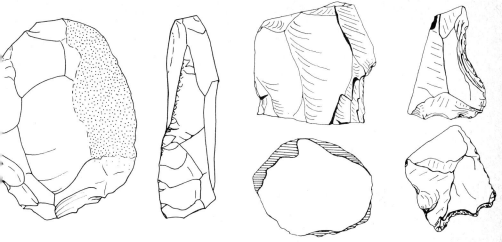

25 Stone implements of the Australian Early Stone Age from the lower level at Kenniff cave, Queensland

wait on the development of advanced navigation by peoples securely based on food-production, notably Antarctica and most islands beyond the continental shelf, were of comparable importance.

By invading the New World the Stone Age hunters laid the foundations of a new and exciting chapter in the cultural history of mankind, but attention will be focused here on the Old World, in particular the territories encircling the Mediterranean and extending from the Atlantic seaboard to Inner Asia. This zone, which significantly coincides with that occupied by Neanderthal man, witnessed the development first of all of Advanced Palaeolithic hunting cultures and in due course of farming and settled life.

Ill. 26

Over the whole of this region new flint industries appeared based on the production, by a particular technique, of blades having more or less parallel flake scars. Anticipations of such blades have been found in Palestine and Syria in deposits earlier than the Levallois-Mousterian previously mentioned. The cores from which

Ill. 27

Oban

Star Carr

Mullerup

Gagarino

Kostienki

La Madeleine
Sauveterre-
la-Lémance

Angles-
sur-l'Anglin

Dolni
Věstonice

Szeleta

La Solutré

Lascaux

Niaux

Altamira

Tuc d'Audoubert

Mas-d'Azil

La Portel

Wady en-Natuf

Jericho

ΛΛΛΛΛΛΛΛ
WWWWW Known final limit of ice sheets

------- Shore line at end of Palæolithic period

26   Important sites in the Advanced Palaeolithic and Mesolithic worlds

Ill. 28

these blades were struck had to be prepared in a fashion
analogous to the tortoise-core of the Levallois technique,
even if for obvious reasons they differed in their elongated
shape. Another technique of flint-working applied commonly enough to blades was blunting the edges of blades
or bladelets by a steep retouch intended either to allow
the finger to exercise pressure without being cut, rather
as in a pen-knife blade, or to facilitate hafting as knife-

27, 28 Advanced Palaeolithic blade tools from the classic site at La Madeleine, France. *Left*, a blade-core, *above*, an end-scraper, a burin and a backed blade

edges or the barbs and tips of weapons with wooden handles. The creation of burins or graving tools with chisel-like working-edges by striking into the length of the blade and detaching one or two small flakes was another feature of Advanced Palaeolithic flint-work.

A striking characteristic of the tool-kit was its diversity both as to form, technique, cultural style and raw material and the dynamic rapidity with which it underwent change in a period of time brief indeed by comparison with that required for barely perceptible changes in earlier times. The much greater variety of well-defined flint forms no doubt reflects in part more complex hunting methods, the multiplication of crafts and the practice of engraving and other forms of art.

In addition to the blade, blunting and burin techniques already mentioned, flint-workers practised edge-trimming and shallow surface flaking. Antler, bone and ivory were systematically worked for the first time into a variety of

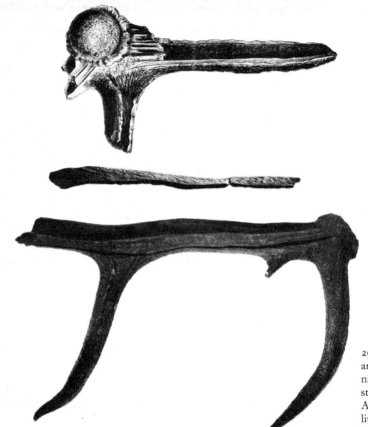

29 The groove and splinter technique applied to stag antler by Advanced Palaeolithic and Mesolithic man

Ill. 29

Ills. 52–54

implements, weapon-heads and ornaments. A number of different techniques were employed; the system of removing splinters from antler and bone by cutting parallel grooves and prising out the intervening portion was discovered very early; flaking, and above all polishing, were used to shape and finish tools; and perforation was carried out to make a variety of batons, needles and ornaments. Another novelty of outstanding importance was the use of hafting, more particularly for hunting gear of different kinds, so that several of the leading forms made of flint, bone or antler were in fact only elements in composite weapons.

30 Rock shelter overlooking the Lower Murray river at Devon Downs, near Adelaide, South Australia

Where caves and rock-shelters were available, as they were in much of France, Britain, Spain, Italy, South and Central Germany, Austria, Greece, south-west Asia and North Africa, they were commonly occupied at this time just as they have been much more recently in Australia. In the case of deep caves people normally lived in the zone near the entrance. By removing the deposits carefully over large enough areas it has sometimes been possible to find traces of nest-like areas within the protection of the cave or shelter as the case may be, as though artificial shelters had been erected under the overhanging rock. In areas without caves, like the whole of South Russia outside the

Ill. 30

31 Reconstruction of a mammoth hunters' dwelling based on finds at Pushkari, near Novgorod-Seversky, South Russia. The dwelling was nearly 40 feet long and 12 feet wide, standing in a shallow pit

Ill. 31

Ill. 32

Crimea, the Caucasus and the Urals, the loess of Moravia or the open plain of North Germany, reliance had to be placed entirely on structures in the open and it needs little imagination to appreciate that during glacial periods in particular these must have been exposed to merciless winds. The mammoth-hunters of this part of Europe, whether on the loess of Moravia or on the river bluffs of South Russia, most commonly lived in dwellings of irregular oval plan, having the floor scooped a few inches into the subsoil. Post-holes have only rarely been observed and there is no sign of elaborate frame-built superstructures; more likely the huts were roofed by earth resting on branches supported by a few uprights wedged against the floor. Another type of structure was apparently used by the Late Glacial hunters of North Germany; in this case animal skins supported on wooden uprights formed a kind of tent and the sides were held down by heavy boulders arranged in a round or pear-shaped setting.

The great advantage of caves and rock-shelters to archaeologists is that they provide stratified sequences of deposits and by excavating a number of these it is often

32 Round hut floor with mammoth tusks uncovered at Dolní Věstonice, Czechoslovakia, under a thick deposit of loess

possible to establish a succession of cultural phases. Since French prehistorians were the first to exploit this possibility at all systematically, it follows that many of the most recognizable assemblages are named after French sites. There is no great harm in this so long as we avoid trying to fit all the finds made since over the whole Advanced Palaeolithic world into the French sequence. There is no warrant for the idea that the succession of cultures were necessarily evolved in France. One needs to keep in mind the whole world of Advanced Palaeolithic man, taking full advantage of radio-carbon dating, to synchronize events in widely separated areas, if one is to

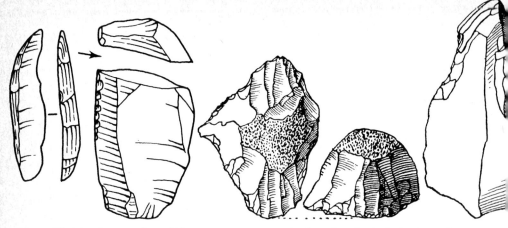

33 Flint implements from Ed Dabba, Cyrenaica; a battered back blade and chisel-like tool with a sharpening flake

34 Aurignacian beaked burin and rostrate scraper

understand even the French sequence. A further point is worth making before we come to review the sequence and that is that we know very little about the process by which cultural fashions spread and cultural changes occurred in Palaeolithic times. When we speak of cultures spreading we do not mean to imply in this context actual movements of peoples or tribes; only that certain techniques and styles were adopted over a wider area.

Ill. 33

One of the oldest Advanced Palaeolithic assemblages known is that first recognized at Ed Dabba and later found overlying Levalloiso-Mousterian layers at Haua Fteah in Cyrenaica, at both of which sites it was dated by radio-carbon to around 38,000 years ago. The flint industry is based on blades and prepared tortoise or disc cores are replaced exclusively by ones resulting from the production of blades. Among forms shaped by secondary flaking are backed blades, one edge of which has been removed by steep retouch, and burins, which display the interesting characteristic of having been sharpened by the removal of a transverse sharpening flake. The evidence from the Haua suggests that the Dabba culture was intrusive into North Africa and if so it can only have come from south-west Asia. It will be interesting to determine when research has gone further, the true geographical extent of this early Advanced Palaeolithic industry. Meanwhile it is interesting to note that a close cousin of the later phase of the Dabba culture, the Emiran, was immediately overlaid in the Palestine cave sequence by thick deposits enclosing traces of a culture termed Aurignacian after the French locality of Aurignac. Recent exploration has shown that flint assemblages of Aurignacian type extended as far east as northern Iraq and Afghanistan and the general pattern of discoveries suggests that it spread into Western Europe by way of the Balkans and Central Europe, a spread that reached as far west as the Pyrenees and Cantabria. Over the whole of this territory Aurignacian flint industries can be diagnosed from the presence of beaked burins and rostrate scrapers and many of the European localities have also yielded split-base bone points, significant both as the earliest standardized artifacts made from bone and as indicating, by implication, the use of hafted weapons. When the Aurignacian culture reached France it impinged upon one already established there, taking its name from the French locality of Chatelperron. Radio-carbon analysis suggests that the Chatelperronian was a laggard and unimportant outlier of the undifferentiated Advanced Palaeolithic world.

The Aurignacian was succeeded in France by the Gravettian, similarly named after a French type-station and likewise intrusive into France. Indeed France seems to have been close to the western limits of the Gravettian, which evidently centred on the South Russian Plain and Central Europe, and may have spread to Italy, France and Spain by way of the head of the Adriatic at a time when this was dry land. Gravettian flint-work differed markedly from the Aurignacian in that it included numerous small pieces made from narrow bladelets and shaped by steep,

35 Aurignacian split-base bone point from Istál-lósköer Höhle, Hungary

53

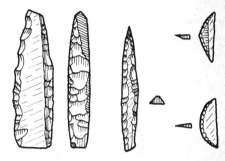

36 Part of a deposit of bones of mammoth, reindeer, horse and other animals discarded by Gravettian hunters at Dolní Věstonice. The overlying material is loess deposited by the winds blowing off the ice-sheets.

37 Gravettian flint-work from Romanelli, Italy

almost vertical retouch; the battered backs were designed to protect the finger when used as knives, or alternatively, represent the blunt side of flints intended to be inserted in wooden shafts or handles. Bone and ivory, though now more freely used, were restricted to a comparatively small range of implements, notably awls or bodkins and probably skin-working tools, as well as a variety of objects of personal adornment. These now included various forms of bead, bracelet and pin, and perforated shells. Another significant feature of the bone and ivory objects was the occasional presence of decorative designs of simple geometrical pattern; frequently these comprised incised strokes arranged as marginal fringes, criss-cross lines and linear chevrons or zig-zags, but mammoth ivories were sometimes decorated by means of large numbers of small pits.

In some respects the most notable products of the culture are the small figurines of women, sometimes referred to flatteringly as 'Venuses', that are found over a wide territory from Italy and France to South Russia and *Ills. 46–48* even Siberia. These figurines measure only a few inches in height and are carved in the round from a variety of stones and from mammoth ivory or modelled from clay *Ills. 38, 39* and hardened in the fire, like pottery, a method especially well seen at Dolní Věstonice in Moravia. Clearly what

38-43 A feature of the Gravettian culture is its figurine art. Some sixty female figurines, the so-called 'Venuses', are known from sites extending from Siberia to Italy and France. Various materials were used such as ivory, bone or soft stone. One example from Moravia was modelled from a pulverized bone and clay mixture which was subsequently hardened by fire like pottery. The figurines commonly show signs of pregnancy. This, like the generous modelling of the buttocks, was no doubt intended to symbolize fertility. The figurine from Dolní Věstonice, *above left*, of which front and back views are shown, exhibits these characteristics, but it is worth noting that the stylized, rod-like,

figurine of mammoth ivory, *opposite right*, was found in the same context at the site. Occasionally the figurines suggest individual persons in their tenderness of execution, as in the tiny ivory head from Brassempouy, *far left*. The facial features are carefully worked, which is unusual, since most of the 'Venus' figurines are faceless, or their faces are masked by the downward cast of the head as with the 'Venus' of Lespugue, *above and right*. This is one of the finest of the French 'Venuses' which was unfortunately damaged on excavation. She wears a curious tapered skirt or apron behind her, an uncommon feature as most of the known figurines are naked as in much of our own modern sculpture interested their makers were the sexual characteristics of the women, full breasts, prominent buttocks and signs of pregnancy; heads were usually shown as mere knobs, though the hair might be represented in conventional fashion and very rarely indeed some features indicated; thighs were shown as plump, but legs were tapered and the feet merely indicated; arms were puny; and clothing, in the rare instances in which the figures were not entirely naked, was as a rule confined to a girdle or fringe. We do not know what purpose these figurines served, but they do far more than reveal primitive man's concern with fertility and the reproduction of his own kind; they epitomize his ability to give expression in symbolic fashion to this concern by means of three-dimensional works of art that remain effective despite their small size. It is particularly interesting to observe that at Dolní Věstonice a symbolic, rod-like figure occurs alongside one in a comparatively naturalistic style. Again, one may compare the schematic engraving on a mammoth tusk from Předmostí in Moravia with the ivory head from Brassempouy in France, carved with such tender feeling as almost to suggest an individual person.

The Solutrean culture, which followed the Gravettian in the French sequence, is marked by leaf-shaped points having shallow surface flaking, at first on one face only, but in due course on both. Surface flaking of this kind, which also appears in Central Europe and South Russia, apparently stems from earlier and specifically Mousterian sources, a reminder that no gulf was fixed between Middle and Advanced Palaeolithic culture any more than between some groups of Neanderthal and Modern men. Equally, there was a clear continuity in Advanced Palaeolithic culture. This is seen in the reappearance of Gravettian features in the later Solutrean and even more vividly in the overall development of Cave Art from France to South Russia.

Ills. 42, 43

Ill. 48

Ill. 44

Ill. 40
Ills. 38, 39
Ill. 45

Ill. 41

Ill. 49

Ill. 50

44, 45 Two contrasting ways of representing the female form are seen in the
torso from Ostrava-Petřkovice, *above*, and
the symbolic figure of a woman from
Předmostí, *right*; both sites are in Moravia.
The tiny torso, it is only 5 centimetres high,
is carefully carved in haematite and compares
with much larger sculptures of modern
European art. The symbolic and stylized
figure of a woman, *right*, is engraved on a
mammoth tusk

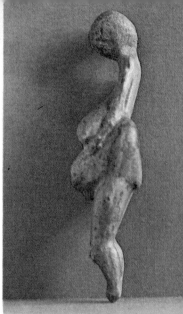

46–48 The mammoth-bone 'Venus' from Kostienki exhibits the characteristic pregnancy, well-developed buttocks and pendulous breasts (*cf. ills. 38, 39, 42, 43*). In the rear view she can be seen to be wearing a fringe or girdle

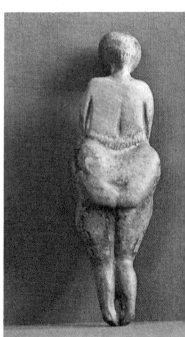

49, 50 The Solutreans introduced a new flint weapon, the pressure-flaked bifacial spear-point, often referred to as a laurel-leaf point. The example, *above*, comes from the type-site of Le Solutré, Dordogne. Fine examples of lance-heads, *right*, have been made by similar techniques among certain groups of North Australian aborigines, who, since the appearance of the white man, have used bottle glass and even telephone insulators, materials even more susceptible to accurate flaking than flint

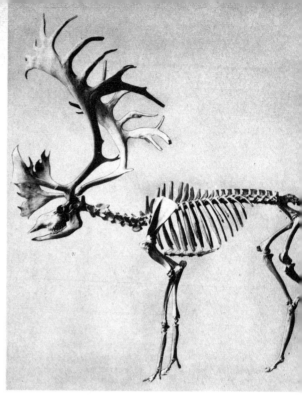

51 Skeleton of a reindeer from Villestofte, Denmark, dating from the close of the Ice Age

Late Glacial Reindeer Hunters

Ill. 51

The final stage of the Advanced Palaeolithic over much of Europe was the appearance of cultures based to a major degree on the specialized hunting of reindeer. This was an animal well adapted to the Late Glacial environment of much of North and even West Europe, one which yielded meat, sinew, skin and antler, all of the greatest value to a community of hunters and one which, because of its gregarious nature can easily be culled when fresh supplies were needed. The best known of the reindeer-hunting cultures is the Late Magdalenian named after the French site of La Madeleine and coinciding with the final stages of the Pleistocene Ice Age. The Magdalenian was centred on France and Cantabria, but penetrated south to Valencia and east to Poland in its earlier stages and in its later ones included parts of south-west Germany; its beginnings may go back to 12000 or even 15000 B C and it lasted down to between 8–9000 B C. It was characterized

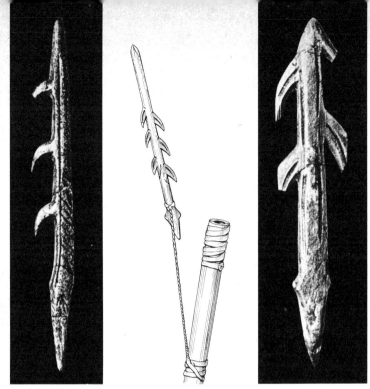

52–54 The 'type-fossil' of the Late Magdalenian culture is the barbed harpoon head, found with single and double barbs. These examples are Late Magdalenian from Le Souci, Dordogne, and the method of hafting them is shown

by the widespread use of antler and bone as raw materials for hunting gear: various types of lance-head and of harpoon-head were made; and spear-throwers hooked at one end to engage the shaft were frequently decorated with naturalistic carvings of horses, ibex and other game animals, as well as birds and fish. The lavish and extremely skilful manner in which such things were ornamented is indeed one of the most notable features of this culture.

Ills. 52–54

Ills. 55, 56

Farther north traces of several other reindeer-hunting groups have been found in deposits of Late Glacial Age. Some of these are represented almost entirely by flint industries, but in the case of the Hamburgian and the Ahrensburgian cultures, both centred on Schleswig-Holstein and extending over substantial parts of the North European Plain, many organic materials have survived in

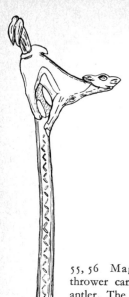

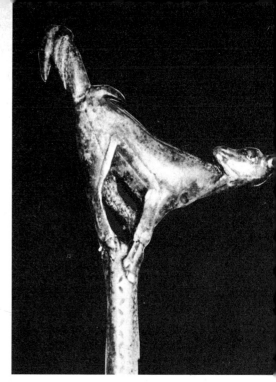

55, 56 Magdalenian spear-thrower carved from reindeer antler. The young ibex at the head is shown in the process of evacuating and the dropping is shaped to form a hook to engage the base of the spear-shaft

waterlogged deposits and we know more about the animals hunted and the equipment used by the hunters. The animal bones recovered from such sites as Meiendorf and Stellmoor show that the Hamburgians and Ahrensburgians alike depended almost entirely on reindeer, so much so that in terms of meat this animal provided something like 99 per cent of requirements, a situation more extreme even than that found for example in Late Magdalenian levels at Petersfels in South Germany, where among the larger mammals reindeer accounted for 640, horse 100, ox 10, red deer 8, and roe deer 6 individuals. In addition to meat, which could of course be dried if necessary, reindeer provided the skins needed for clothing and tents, sinews for thread and lines for hunting gear, bones and antler for tools and weapons and teeth for ornaments. By establishing close association with a reindeer herd a group of hunters was able to secure what was in effect a walking larder and a source of supply for raw materials needed in technology. In order to maintain such a symbiotic relationship the hunters had necessarily to move with the reindeer herds, keeping to the shelter of forests in winter and only moving north to the tunnel valleys of the subarctic for the summer grazing.

As might be expected the equipment recovered from the Schleswig-Holstein sites relates primarily to the hunting of reindeer and the processing of their skins, bones and antlers. Both groups used harpoons or detachable spearheads made from splinters cut by the ancient groove technique out of reindeer antler, analogous to but differing markedly in style from those of the Late Magdalenians. The burins and pronged tools used to cut the grooves in antler and undercut the spongy tissue in the interior of the shaft, making it possible to detach intervening splinters, were among the commonest flint artifacts. Both groups made projectile points. The Hamburgians probably mounted their shouldered points as the heads of spearheads or darts, but the Ahrensburgians were certainly using the bow-and-arrow, since we find not only delicate tanged points, but pinewood arrow-shafts and fore-shafts and even grooved sandstone rubbers for smoothing these. The Ahrensburgians, like the Gravettians of Central Europe long before, made clubs from the beams of reindeer antlers, with the brow-tine cut off short and bevelled to form a stout blade, and these, to judge from holes in some of the reindeer skulls, were used to despatch wounded quarry. The importance of animal skins to people ignorant of textiles and living in a cool climate need hardly be stressed and it is not surprising to find that scraping-tools were among the commonest types of worked flint.

The success of the Advanced Palaeolithic peoples as hunters, who took every advantage of the almost ideal conditions for grazing animals that prevailed over much of the ice-free territories of Europe and contiguous zones during Late Glacial times, and who in the closing

Ill. 29

phases seem to have ensured their food supplies by establishing close associations with individual reindeer herds, is reflected in the art which more than anything else must serve as their memorial. Advanced Palaeolithic art is indeed far more than this; it gives us a priceless insight into the psychic life not only of our forebears but of ourselves.

CHAPTER FOUR

The Cave Artists

Although, where found together, the two main classes of Advanced Palaeolithic art help to illuminate one another, it is convenient to distinguish between chattel art, that is art applied to the small objects normally to be found in archaeological deposits, whether in caves or in the open, and parietal art, the art restricted to the walls, roofs and occasionally floors of caves and rock-shelters. Geographically it is evident that parietal art is limited by the availability of suitable caves, whereas chattel art is likely to be found much more evenly over the territories occupied by the Advanced Palaeolithic cultures. Another limiting factor is uneven exploration. For instance it has long been recognized that female figurines occur not only in south-western Europe, where they were first recognized, but also in Italy, Central Europe, South Russia and even Siberia; and indeed that their main weight of distribution lies in Eastern rather than Western Europe. In the case of parietal art it remains true that France south of the Loire and west of the Rhine, together with the Spanish provinces of Cantabria, Old Castile and Andalusia, constitutes the main core. Yet in recent years discovery has revealed an important new province in Italy in the neighbourhood of Tivoli, near Rome, in the areas of Otranto and Palermo, and on the small island of Levanzo off the north coast of

Ill. 60

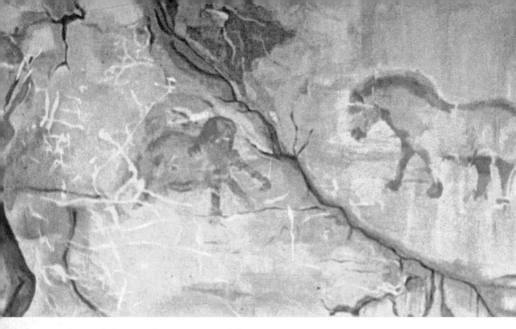

57 Copy of the most important panel from the cave paintings found in the Kapovaya cave on the south bend of the Bielaya river, southern Urals. The original painting is located some 150 metres underground from the actual cave entrance

58 Abstract finger drawings done in the red clay on the rock surface in the cave of La Baume Latrone, Gard

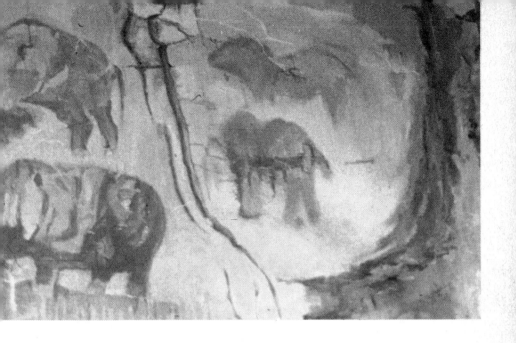

59   Naturalistic engraving of a bison from La Grèze, Dordogne. Here the artist has tried to overcome the problem of foreshortening the head and horns

Sicily. More dramatic still has been the recent revelation of the painted friezes in the Kapovaya cave at the south bend of the Bielaya River in the South Urals, since at one blow this extends the distribution of parietal art to the eastern frontier of Europe. The paintings, which comprise several dozen animals, including above all deer, steppe horse, mammoth and cave bear, have been executed in yellow, red, deep brown and charcoal colours. What makes them of such exceptional interest is that they are situated approximately 150 metres from the entrance to the narrow cave, reminding us in this respect, as well as in their style, of those long known from the Franco-Cantabrian 'sanctuaries'. Few illustrations could be more striking of the need to take a broad view of Palaeolithic cave art, the kind of view from which we have for some time been accustomed to regard the female figurines or the flint and bone industries of the Gravettian culture.

Cave art took the form of engraving and painting, either separately or in conjunction; reliefs made by cutting away the rock to varying depths; doodling on clay films on wall, ceiling or floor; and modelling clay figures in full relief. Colouring matter consisted of various kinds of ochre, manganese and charcoal. This would either be mixed with animal fat to bind it together and applied by means of the finger or some kind of brush or pad, or blown on in the form of powder or drawn on direct by a stick of charcoal. Flint burins were used for engraving and stone picks or punches, as well as flint

tools, for carving. Outlines on stone plaques from the cave deposits may in some cases have served for practice. The existence of well-defined regional groups, as well as of a chronological succession of styles, suggests that the art was transmitted from masters to pupils. It is reasonable to think that those initiated more fully into the art were men naturally gifted in that direction, but it would be quite wrong to imagine that societies so small and with

60, 61 *Left*, engraved deer from Levanzo, Sicily: the problem of foreshortening has here been overcome in the graceful way in which the animal's head is turned back. *Above*, an engraving of a bison on a pebble from Laugerie Basse, Dordogne. Outlines such as this probably served as preparatory sketches, for practice, or as a convenient way in which the rough sketches could be carried in the manner of a 'pattern book'

so primitive a basis of subsistence could have supported full-time artists. On the other hand hunters would be likely to enjoy periods of leisure; and these might have been more prolonged than, for example, among primitive peasant communities.

Before considering further the content of the art and pondering on its meaning it is important to review in summary outline its basic chronology. Breuil held that the art passed through two major cycles, but most prehistorians now believe in a straightforward sequence.

Period I (*c.* 30–23000 BC). According to modern French prehistorians there was for a lengthy period no assured parietal art, only tentative engravings and paintings applied to bone and plaques of stone. Little more than scribbles came from Chatelperronian and Aurignacian deposits. The first co-ordinated silhouettes of animals were executed by people of evolved Aurignacian and early Gravettian culture. Yet, however tentative,

62 Stylized engraving of a vulva. Style I, La Ferrassie, Dordogne

63 Relief carving of a boar, followed by a wild horse. Style III, Le Roc de Sers, Charente

representations like those at La Ferrassie and Abri Cellier established the basic pattern of the art, in that they combined animal forms with symbolic signs, including dots and vulva.

Ill. 62

Period II (c. 23–17000 BC). This opens with the evolved stage of Gravettian culture in France and continues into the early Solutrean. It is characterized above all by animal silhouettes on cave walls that depend first and foremost on a strongly defined cervical-dorsal curve to which the head, limbs and lower part are, so to speak, added. Excellent representations of this phase are known from Pair-non-Pair and La Grèze.

Ill. 59

Period III (c. 17–13000 BC). This corresponds with the Late Solutrean and the partly overlapping Early Magdalenian. It saw the gradual loss of the curved profile of back and neck and the beginnings of the depiction of movement, even though this was indicated by no more than the displacement of such features as legs. Great advances were also made at this time in the mastery of technique in painting, a mastery well displayed at Lascaux. The period also witnesses a remarkable develop-

Ill. 65

ment in the art of relief sculpture executed on the limestone wall of the actual living area. The technique of carving indeed reached a peak at this time, though the style remained 'archaic'; for instance, the carvers of the splendid reliefs of Le Roc de Sers made the bodies huge in relation to heads and hoofs, a convention which, however 'primitive' from a photographic viewpoint, admirably conveyed the force and *élan* of the bison.

Ill. 63

Period IV (c. 13–8000 BC) falls into two phases. In the earlier, corresponding broadly with Magdalenian III–IV, animal figures retain certain features of the archaic cannon, notably a disproportion between frontal and rear parts and between body and feet. On the other hand, the paintings at Font de Gaume, Castillo and Altamira display finer modelling, giving something more of the effect of volume, a feature which may well show influence from the tradition of relief carving carried forward from the preceding period, though now, as in the horses of Angles-sur-l'Anglin or Cap Blanc, executed in a more naturalistic style. At this time also there was a marked increase in mobiliary art, notably displayed in the splendid

Ills. 55, 56

series of antler batons and spear-throwers from Magdalenian deposits. Study of these shows that, along with closer fidelity to nature as regards anatomy and proportion, the artists of this time had reduced such details as eyes, horns, cheeks, hair and hoofs to a series of conventions. The Late Magdalenians made a great advance in the naturalistic rendering of individual animals; dropping all but essential detail they succeeded in imparting a real feeling of movement. Good examples of this style are to be found at La Madeleine itself, at Isturitz,

Ill. 64

Teyjat, Limeuil, Le Portel, and at sites in the outlying provinces of South Germany, Switzerland and Belgium. The decoration of small objects was if anything even commoner, reflecting above all the exuberance of reindeer hunters at the very peak of their achievement. In a sense therefore the Late Magdalenian artists, though marking the culmination of art many thousands of years old, were celebrating the adjustment of an advanced hunting culture to a particular set of environmental conditions. When these changed with dramatic suddenness at the end of the Ice Age, the economic infrastructure of the Magdalenian life collapsed and with it the art of the caves.

In trying to assess the meaning and significance of Palaeolithic art, we must at all costs avoid judging it in terms of our modern culture. If we wish to understand the attitude of Palaeolithic man, we must turn for one instant to a society like that of the Australian aborigines. Among these people art is not an amusement or a means of self-expression; it is an adjustment to the rites and ceremonies connected with birth, death, fertility and the propitiation of evil forces. When the aborigines of central

Ill. 67

Australia engrave and paint rocks they do so as part of a ritual that may involve mime, dancing and the recitation of legends, a major aim of which is to reassure society at large and enhance the confidence of its individual

64 Painted outline of a horse. Style IV, Le Portel, Ariège

members. They seek to ensure rain, the well-being of the animals and plants on which they depend and the increase both of these and of their own kind. The Upper Palaeolithic hunting peoples of Western Europe were also preoccupied with the need for food and the need to perpetuate themselves. They were concerned, as they might well be, considering the primitive nature of their equipment, with success in the hunt, on which they depended for their only important source of food and clothing. The Upper Palaeolithic cave-dwellers suffered common enough anxieties; their special claim on our attention is the manner in which they sought to resolve them through the medium of art.

On the other hand we can hardly overlook the fact that the cave artists were indeed artists and ones with whom in the present climate of appreciation it is not difficult to establish sympathy. One of the difficulties to be faced

65   Painting of a great black bison, in Style II, on the wall at the entrance to the main gallery
Lascaux, Dordogne. Incised across its back are signs variously interpreted as male symbols

arts. The smaller horse looking left was painted later because the engraved outline of its rear
verlies that of the bison. Symbolic signs are also to be seen immediately in front of the bison

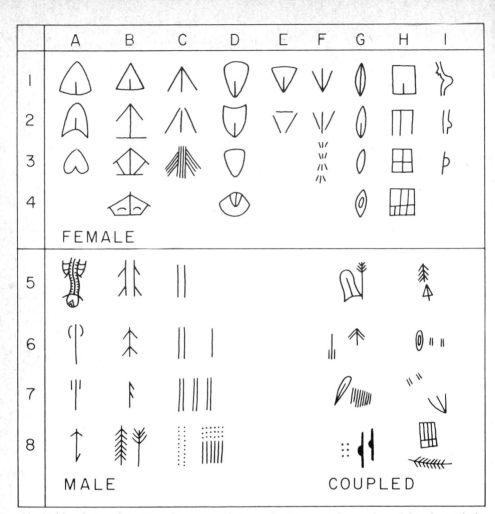

66   Table of signs from French cave art that may be interpreted as male and female symbols, either separately or coupled

when reading books about cave art written by elderly prehistorians is that they tend to judge the productions of Palaeolithic man in terms of their fidelity to natural forms in the manner of academic artists of a former age. It is true enough that as their technique developed the cave artists managed to achieve a more life-like appearance for the animals they depicted, but modern taste might still prefer the archaic style in which natural appearance

67 Sam of Milingimbi, Arnhem Land, painting a legendary design on bark. Note how absorbed he is in this task

was, from an academic point of view, 'distorted'; even at the apogee of naturalism in the later phase of Period IV the Palaeolithic artists dispensed with all but the most necessary detail and rendered even this conventionally.

It has already been suggested that the capacity to symbolize underlay the articulate speech on which the development of human culture must so largely have depended. There can hardly be any doubt that much of

70 Limestone relief carving of a woman, grasping a horn in her right hand, from Laussel, Dordogne. The horn, like the woman, is a symbol of fertility ▷

68, 69   The negatives of human hands, with their fingers bent back, *above left*, were made by outlining in red and black paint. They are from the cave of Gargas, Hautes Pyrénées. *Below* are negatives of human hands on the wall and ceiling of a rock-shelter at Toombs, New South Wales

Palaeolithic art was symbolic in intent. The notable use in both negative and positive form of the human hand, the organ that reaches furthest, makes and uses weapons and implements and serves in gesture to command, implore, greet, threaten and submit, is surely significant.

Even more definite is the existence both in the parietal and chattel art of numerous signs, many of which can be shown with a fair degree of certainty to symbolize the male and female sexes and conjunctions of these. The sexual nature of certain more or less pictographic signs is not to be doubted and by comparing their forms one can see that numerous others are either simplifications or complications of the basic ones. The numerous occasions on which 'Male' and 'Female' signs can be placed in juxtaposition only help to confirm their interpretation as symbols of sex.

The symbolic nature of the small figurines of women from Gravettian sites has already been stressed. In some ways even more striking are the much larger relief carvings dating from the transition from Periods III–IV and concentrated in the Perigord, where they are exposed directly to the open air or at least in locations to some degree lit by daylight. One might particularly single out in this respect the frieze on the limestone wall of Angles-sur-l'Anglin, Vienne, which shows only the hips and thighs of female forms viewed from the front; or even

more pointedly the obese woman from Laussel in the Dordogne holding in the right hand a horn, itself an emblem of fertility, not to mention the birth scene shown on a separate slab from the same site. On the male side one might recall the so-called satyr of Le Portel in the Ariège, utilizing a stalagmitic column as his erect male organ, or the clay phalloi from a recess in the cave of Tuc-d'Audoubert not far from the clay models of a male bison following a female, a motif repeated in the engraving of a bull following a cow at Teyjat.

It is even claimed with some show of plausibility by the eminent French prehistorian André Leroi-Gourhan that the animals that make up the main element in parietal art may also have a specifically sexual connotation. Analysis of over two thousand animal representations in the Franco-Cantabrian art and of their locations and associations suggests that the animals shown, or at least many of them, were divided symbolically into two moities, male and female, the former including horses, ibex and deer, the latter bison, cattle and mammoths. In fact some French authorities see the essence of Palaeolithic religion, as expressed in the art, revolving round the opposition and complementarity of male and female essence and values, expressed symbolically in representations of humans and animals and in signs. Here again the hypothesis is supported by the positioning of the representations; the depths and zones near the entrance are dedicated to men, male signs and animals of the male moiety; whereas symbols of the female sex are concentrated in the central zone though significantly accompanied by a certain number of male symbols.

The interpretation of Palaeolithic cave art as if its main function was to provide magical power for the food-quest is no longer tenable. Indeed the theory that its driving power was hunting-magic was based on two concepts, neither of which can any longer be sustained, at least in their full vigour, namely that the cave artists were intent on naturalistic rendering of detail and that this detail can be validly interpreted by invoking superficial parallels with selected elements of modern primitive culture. In point of fact several of the most telling details of the art can equally well be interpreted in terms of sexual symbolism. Thus, both the 'tectiforms', formerly interpreted as huts or traps, and the 'claviforms' once classed as clubs or throwing-sticks are convincingly accepted by Leroi-Gourhan as female symbols. Again, the

Ill. 71

73, 74 Prehistoric cave art was largely ▷
zoomorphic. Many of the animals painted or
engraved in the caves were executed with
sensitive feeling. The polychrome young
deer *opposite*, from the ceiling at Altamira, is
a masterpiece of this kind. Many of the rock-
paintings also convey a great sense of
vigour and movement. The archer dis-
charging his bow at a leaping ibex, *opposite
below*, from Remigia in eastern Spain con-
veys the action of the scene with the minimum of fuss

71, 72 Numerous signs and symbols of probably sexual connotation occur in the cave art (*see
ill. 66*). Some appear as separate designs, as the example *above* from Castillo, Santander. Others
overlie representations of animals, as the bison *below*, engraved on clay from Niaux, Ariège

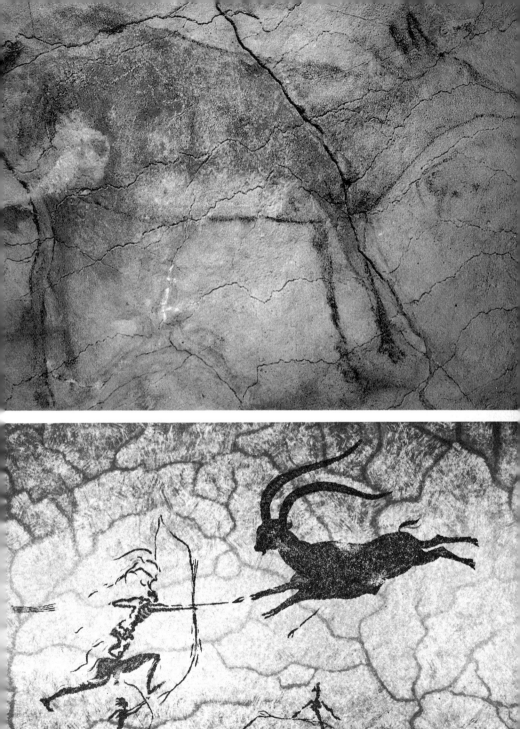

Ill. 72
'wounds' of the famous bison of Niaux can as well be interpreted as vulva and the 'arrows' as male organs; indeed a bison on the central panel at Bernifal actually carries oval vulva signs instead of wounds and male baton signs in place of darts or arrows.

Whichever explanation one chooses to adopt, whether one still adheres to the time-honoured theory that representations were made in order to gain control over the animals needed for food by means of sympathetic magic, or whether one regards them as in some way representing the antithesis between the male and female principles, the certain fact is that the Palaeolithic artists *Ill. 73* were concerned first and foremost with delineating wild animals. If we except the small figurines and reliefs of woman, the human figure is comparatively rare and then only schematically represented. Palaeolithic man was interested above all in the animals which provided him *Ill. 74* with meat. His art was to a large extent zoomorphic. Before he had domesticated them and made them slaves of his will, early man revered animals. Indeed it is only in terms of such veneration that we can inderstand the intensity of feeling with which he depicted them; Palaeolithic man was not delineating items for his menu so much as his gods. The fact that he killed them for food did not affect the issue and he killed them, if we judge from the feelings of existing peoples at a comparable level of technology, with reluctance, as a crude necessity. Indeed so close did early man feel to his food animals that he made no clear distinction between them and himself. *Ills. 75–79* In the representation of masked figures with animal heads, antlers and skins strapped over human forms, we need not recognize hunting magic but rather a deeply felt community between man and the animals he hunted for his food.

As we have already seen in relation to the Gravettians, the artistic ebullience of the Advanced Palaeolithic

75, 76 The stag antler mask, *above*, was found at the Mesolithic hunter-fisher site of Star Carr, East Riding, Yorkshire. A more recent parallel for such a mask or head-dress is seen in the eighteenth-century engraving *right*, of a Tungu 'shaman'

hunters extended to the ornamentation of their personal possessions and this was specially true of the Magdalenians who, in addition to decorating more or less lavishly a variety of artifacts mainly of reindeer antler, even went so far as to emphasize by engraved lines the barbs and stems of their harpoon-heads. The ornamentation of the person was another way in which the Gravettians and their successors displayed their aesthetic awareness. A variety of beads, including spacers for multiple necklaces, pendants, pins, bracelets and anklets were made from materials ranging from bone, ivory, stone, amber, brown coal and fish vertebrae to fired clay and shells. It is worth emphasizing that some of the latter are among the earliest

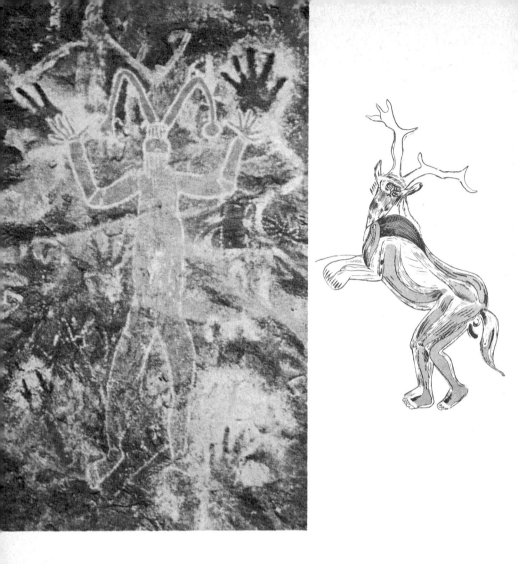

77–79   The wearing of a horned head-dress (*see ills. 75, 76*), is a very widespread custom among primitive peoples. *Above left*, wearing such a head-dress is a painting of a ritual postulant or mythical figure on a rock-shelter at St Vidgeon, south-east Arnhem Land, Australia. The best known prehistoric representation of a horned head-dress being worn is that on the famous 'sorcerer' from Les Trois Frères, Ariège, see *above right* in a reconstruction drawing and *opposite*, the original

80 Magdalenian eyed needles for sewing animal skins and pendants made from bone, a tooth and a shell

Ill. 80

Ill. 81

81 Skull with an ornamental shell 'cap' from a burial in the Grotte des Enfants, Grimaldi cave, Monaco

indications of distant 'trade', a pointer to the power of conspicious consumption as an economic force even in the Ice Age. Certain hints in the cave-art and the presence of numerous finely eyed needles in Magdalenian deposits suggest that sewn skin clothing was worn out of doors, as is still the case over a large part of the Arctic zone. To judge from the position of shells and other objects in their ceremonial burials, they were laid to rest fully clothed, sprinkled with ochre, and adorned with the ornaments on which they clearly set store in life.

CHAPTER FIVE

From Hunters to Farmers

The close of the Pleistocene Ice Age and the beginning of Neothermal climate ushered in the world in which we live in more senses than one. For one thing it witnessed geographical changes that shaped the environment familiar to us from historic times. In some territories the transition was more gradual, but in others, notably those on the margins of ecological zones, it was sufficiently sudden to have affected the conditions for human life in dramatic fashion. In some respects the most notable changes were those involved in the contraction of ice-sheets which occurred as temperatures rose. For example quite large tracts of north-western Europe were newly exposed for human settlement. The return of melt-water to the ocean and the recovery of land formerly depressed by the weight of ice-sheets brought about changes of sea-level great enough to alter the shape of the land. Again, the rise of temperature which brought about the melting of the ice altered the conditions of life for animals and plants. As a result forest trees spread over the open landscape and red deer, elk and aurochs replaced reindeer, bison and horse. Farther south the displacement of climatic zones must also have produced their effects and these may even have assisted the economic transformation that first gave rise to farming in south-west Asia.

Mesolithic Hunter-fishers in Europe

Changes in the environment on the scale indicated for northern Europe must have affected profoundly the conditions of life of the hunting peoples of the Advanced Palaeolithic world and not least in what is now Temperate Europe. It might be thought axiomatic that the increase of temperature that marked the end of the Ice Age would have made for more congenial conditions of life. This was true in the sense that in a region like Scandinavia in particular additional tracts of land became available for human settlement. On the other hand until temperatures had risen enough for deciduous forests to replace ones of pine and birch there was no question of being able to increase the supply of food by farming. The indigenous peoples had therefore to adapt themselves to hunting, fishing and gathering in a predominantly forested environment. In doing so they had to face harder conditions. The spread of forests reduced drastically the area available to grazing animals, the main source of food and even raw materials of the Advanced Palaeolithic peoples. As we have already seen, the Late Glacial vegetation, which finds no exact parallel today, combining as it did elements of tundra, steppe and alpine flora, supported herds of reindeer that made it possible for the later Magdalenians, Hamburgians and the like to practise a type of herd-hunting of a very special kind and one that gave them a plentiful supply of most basic necessities. For such people and their immediate successors Neothermal conditions were little short of catastrophic. As the forests closed in grazing areas were reduced to forest glades, lake margins, river valleys and upland zones beyond the tree-line. The available grazing was not merely reduced in area; what remained was broken up into comparatively small, discrete patches.

Early man responded in two ways; he had in the first place to adapt his hunting methods to the pursuit of

82 Maglemosian wooden bows with shaped grip from Holmegaard, Denmark

83 An Australian aborigine family on a hunting trek. Note how the woman carries the domestic
equipment leaving the man unencumbered with his weapons ready for use

individual animals rather than herds and to this end he
made much greater use of the bow, a device which only
came in during the closing phases of the Ice Age. The
earliest bows so far known are those from the bog of
Holmegaard in Denmark. These were self bows about the
height of a man made from a single length of springy
wood like elm or yew and shaped with carefully made
grips near the middle of the stave. Arrow-shafts sometimes exceeded a metre in length and were nocked at one
end to engage the bowstring, as well as being fletched
with feathers to steady the flight and pointed and barbed
by microliths. Secondly, he had no choice but to widen
the range of his quest for food. Instead of being able to

Ill. 133

Ill. 82

Ill. 84

Ill. 85

93

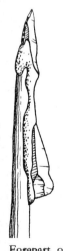

84 Forepart and base of a Maglemosian wooden arrowshaft from Vinkelmose, Denmark. The tip is a slot for a microlithic point and the base is notched to engage the bow-string. The binding was to hold the feathering required to steady the flight of the arrow

Ills. 88, 90

Ills. 86, 87
Ill. 91

concentrate on reindeer he had to revert to hunting a broad range of herbivorous big game, elk, red deer, roe deer, aurochs and wild pig. Moreover he had to supplement this by pursuing smaller land game, wildfowl and fish, and increasingly by exploiting the resources of the seashore, including shellfish, crustacea, stranded sea-mammals and inshore fish.

Over many parts of south-western and southern Europe the culture of the Mesolithic inhabitants was in all measurable respects inferior to that of their Advanced Palaeolithic forebears. The ebullience and verve of the Magdalenian hunters were based on altogether exceptional conditions which came to an end with the Ice Age itself. If the shellfish eaters of the Tagus estuary or of the coast of Morbihan had solved the problem of survival they had not, to judge from what they left behind them, much energy left to enjoy their lives. On the other hand the Mesolithic inhabitants of the North European Plain, the Maglemosians as they have been termed, after a locality (*magle mose*, meaning a big bog) at Mullerup on the Danish island of Zealand, seem to have enjoyed a richer culture. Over the whole of their territories from eastern England to the Soviet Union they were fond of living close to lakes; at Starr Carr near Scarborough in Yorkshire they even went to the trouble of constructing a platform of birch brushwood so as to be near the water's edge. Largely because of this habit an unusually large amount of organic evidence has survived, so that in general we know more about their food supply and material culture than we do about other Mesolithic groups. The Maglemosians lived mainly by hunting; in addition to the bow-and-arrow they used spears with barbed antler and bone heads. They also fished, taking pike by spearing them, also using lines with barbless bone hooks, and nets made

85 Forepart of a Mesolithic arrow from Løshult, Sweden, showing a microlithic tip and barb held in position by resin

94

86, 87 Shell-mounds bear witness of the importance of the seashore as a source of food during the Stone Age. *Above* is a prehistoric Danish shell-mound, *below* an example in use by Australian aborigines in Arnhem Land

88, 89 The method of throwing a spear using a spear-thrower has not changed basically among primitive peoples since spear-throwers were introduced in Magdalenian times (*see ills. 55, 56*). *Above*, an Australian aborigine is shown, poised just prior to his throw, the spear-thrower is clearly seen. *Left*, Mesolithic barbed spearhead of stag antler from the bed of the North Sea

from bast weighted by stones and supported by wooden or bark floats. Fowling was also carried on and nuts and fruits were gathered in season. No domestic animals were kept except dogs, and of course no crops were grown and no pottery was made. Not much is known about Maglemosian dwellings, but traces have been found in Danish bogs of roughly rectangular huts with bark floors and walls of small branches rammed into the ground and pulled together at the top to form a roof.

A feature of Maglemosian culture was the attack upon forest trees. These were cut down and utilized by means of primitive axes and adzes made of flint mounted on

90, 91 Mesolithic man caught fish by using lines, spears or nets. *Above* is an Australian aborigine taking fish using a long, three-pronged spear, resembling those used by Mesolithic man in northern and north-western Europe or the Levant. *Below*, is a plaited fish-trap, or wheel, from Holbaek, Jutland, of Stone Age date. Similar traps continued in use down to modern times in some parts of Europe, often in conjunction with weirs

92 Mesolithic pine-bark floats and sections of a bast fish-net found at Antrea, Finland. Seine nets with floats are still used by fishermen in North Europe today

Ills. 93–95

Ills. 96, 97

Ill. 98

antler sleeves into which wooden handles were set. From the wood obtained in this way they made a variety of handles, bows, paddles and dug-out canoes. Great use was also made of antler and bone taken from the animals they killed in the hunt. From these they made mattock-heads, holders for axes and adzes, skin-working tools, fish-hooks, netting needles, awls and many barbed spear-heads. The impression of a vigorous culture is heightened by the art. There were no caves in the region and so no cave art, but, particularly in the West Baltic area, the Maglemosians decorated implements, weapons, perforated batons and amulets with lightly incised lines and neatly drilled pits; and occasionally they carved lumps of amber into animal shapes. In addition to geometrical patterns of an abstract character, they introduced conventionalized

93 Birch trees felled by Mesolithic man at the site of Star Carr, Yorkshire, *c.* 7500 BC

94, 95 Maglemosian mattock of elk antler from Star Carr, Yorkshire, and an adze-head of flint mounted in a stag-antler 'sleeve' from Denmark

96, 97 Mesolithic wooden paddle from Duvensee, Schleswig-Holstein, *left*, and, *below*, a tree-trunk hollowed out to form a dug-out canoe from Pesse, Holland, *c.* 6400 BC

animal motifs and anthropomorphic designs. These resembled ones painted on stone pebbles found in the cave of Mas d'Azil in the Ariège, from layers immediately overlying those of the Late Magdalenian reindeer hunters of southern France. The Azilian pebbles probably served the same kind of purpose as the sacred stones of the Australian aborigines which could only be seen by initiated men. Like their Advanced Palaeolithic forebears the Mesolithic peoples practised a variety of forms of ceremonial burial. The coast midden-dwellers of Morbihan buried their dead in skin cloaks fastened by bone pins and sometimes protected them with stone slabs and crowned them with stag antlers symbolic perhaps of new life. Reference will be made later to the remarkable cult of head-burial practised in South Germany (pp. 117–18).

The closing phases of the European Mesolithic were marked by the growth of coastal cultures in which the resources of the interior were supplemented to varying degrees by the hunting of sea-mammals, the catching of

98 Amber, found occurring naturally on the shores of the Baltic, was prized in prehistoric and later times and traded over long distances. It was often made into beads or carved into animal forms by Maglemosian artists. The brown bear comes from Resen and the silhouette elk-head from Egemarke

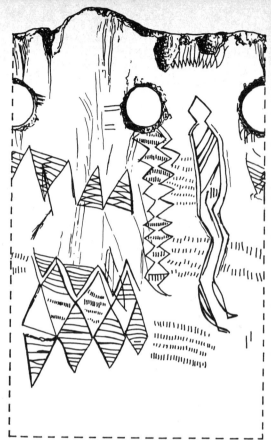

99–101 The Mesolithic hunters lived in forests or near water. Their artistic feelings were expressed in more or less schematic, but doubtless symbolic engravings on tools and weapons, mainly of bone. *Left* is a detail of a stag-antler mattock from Jordløse engraved with a human figure, with, *above*, an expanded drawing of the entire decoration; *below*, five human figures in an enigmatic scene engraved on a wild oxbone from Ryemarksgaard, Denmark

102, 103 The painted pebbles from a Mesolithic level at Mas d'Azil, Ariège, *right*, bear human symbols. They were obviously of deep ritual significance. *Above*, sacred stones, water-smoothed river pebbles, are being shown to initiated male aborigines in Arnhem Land. The pebbles do not occur locally and were originally brought a long distance. They are too sacred to be seen by women and are normally kept secreted in the bag *left*

sea fish and the gathering of molluscs. This can be well seen in the northern parts of Denmark where large numbers of coastal middens are known, on the coast of West Sweden, round the Norwegian coast as far as the northernmost province of Finnmark, on either side of the North Channel in Ulster and western Scotland and on what are now islands off the coast of Morbihan. By around 3000 BC Neolithic peasants were beginning to spread into

Ill. 86

103

104, 105   *Above*, a hollow-ground axe of Circumpolar or Arctic type and *left*, a spearhead slotted to hold flint insets (*cf. ills. 120, 121*) from Bussjö mosse, Scania, Sweden

the old Mesolithic territories round the West Baltic Sea and the hunter-fishers were in due course absorbed by the farming communities that sprang up to exploit the new form of economy.

The Mesolithic inhabitants of Europe were epipalaeolithic in the sense that they carried on an economy based on hunting, fishing and gathering and practised a technology in large measure Advanced Palaeolithic in origin. Yet they can rightly claim a certain measure of independence. In the archaeological record they are marked by a number of traits. Some, like the transversely sharpened axes and adzes and the slotted bone knives and spearheads of the Maglemosian cycle, were restricted to a comparatively small part of Europe. Others, including barbless bone fish-hooks and a wealth of microliths made by a special notch technique and intended in many cases to serve as barbs or tips of projectiles, were of more widespread occurrence. Then there is the distinctive role of providing continuity between Palaeolithic and formally Neolithic societies. Over much of Europe they prepared the way for the spread of Neolithic farming economy when ecological conditions were ripe. They colonized extensive areas previously occupied by ice-sheets, discovered many of the natural resources of the area, including the flint of South Scandinavia, initiated a more settled way of life in some coastal territories and provided a significant element in the ethnic composition of the farming communities that in due course grew up in

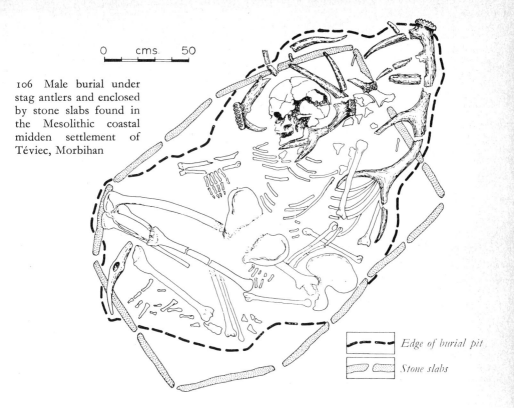

0   cms.   50

106 Male burial under stag antlers and enclosed by stone slabs found in the Mesolithic coastal midden settlement of Téviec, Morbihan

– – – *Edge of burial pit*

Stone slabs

different parts of the continent. In the arctic and sub-arctic tracts of northern Scandinavia and Russia, beyond the northern margin of the deciduous forest, hunter-fishers continued to exist long after farming culture had been established farther south. Indeed no sharp boundary can be drawn in the Stone Age between the zone of hunter-fishers and that of fully fledged peasants. For instance in European Russia the Tripolye peasants who practised a form of mixed husbandry and lived in substantial villages occupied the rich black earth of the Ukraine. Beyond this and extending to the upper reaches of the Volga we enter the territory of peoples who combined stock-raising with vigorous hunting, fishing and trapping activities. The material equipment of these people was formally Neolithic; they made pottery decorated by incised, comb-stamped and cord-impressed patterns and made finely polished

107 Comb and pit marked pot with a frieze of swimming water-birds from Carelia

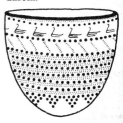

105

108 Profile of a reindeer engraved natural size on an almost vertical wall of rock close to a waterfall at Böla in Nord-Tröndelag, Norway. The frequent siting of engravings by water may reflect a concern with fertility

◁ 109 Bone harpoon head found with the skeleton of a Ringed Seal in a clay deposit at Norrköping, Sweden

flint axes and large numbers of polished stone battle-axes. Farther north and east, beyond the extreme limit of deciduous forest, not even stock-raising could be practised and the circumpolar peoples of the pine and birch forests and the open tundra relied exclusively on the age-old sources of wild food. It is interesting to see that many of their implements used in catching, as indeed those of the hunters and stock-raisers farther south, had evidently been developed from Mesolithic prototypes. The rock-engravings of north-west Norway, indeed, remind us distantly of Advanced Palaeolithic cave art, even if in

110, 111 Reindeer photographed in early morning light in Swedish Lappland. They have been herded together for branding. The way in which the animals appear in early morning light may have suggested the outline engravings both of Circumpolar (*cf. ill. 108*) and French Cave Art. *Below*, an elk hunt is in progress

112 Stone mace-head carved into the form of an elk's head from Hvittis, Finland

Ills. 112–114

style they are quite distinct. At the opposite end of the spectrum the influence of the Arctic animal style, most commonly expressed in wood or stone carving of animal heads, can be detected in the art of the Eurasiatic nomads and even of the settled peoples of China. The circumpolar peoples remind us that in environments hostile to the introduction of farming under primitive conditions the basically Mesolithic economy was the only one viable. Again there is no reason to think that their life was in any sense inferior to that of their peasant neighbours with whom they traded and from whom they borrowed the art of potting – their art and the quality of some of their artifacts might even suggest the contrary. Indeed, in some respects they showed themselves remarkably inventive in adapting to the circumpolar environment. For instance, the skin boat depicted in some of their rock-engravings was well adapted to waters with floating ice, as is illus-

Ills. 115, 116
Ills. 117–119

trated by the Eskimo *umiak* and *kayak* of today. Again the sledge and ski were both invented by the Stone Age hunters of northern Eurasia to exploit the possibilities of rapid movement over snow for hunting as well as for travel and transport.

The Transition to Farming in south-west Asia

The situation in south-west Asia was entirely different. Whereas for the reindeer hunters of north-western Europe the onset of Neothermal conditions implied a reversion from specialized herd-hunting to the more

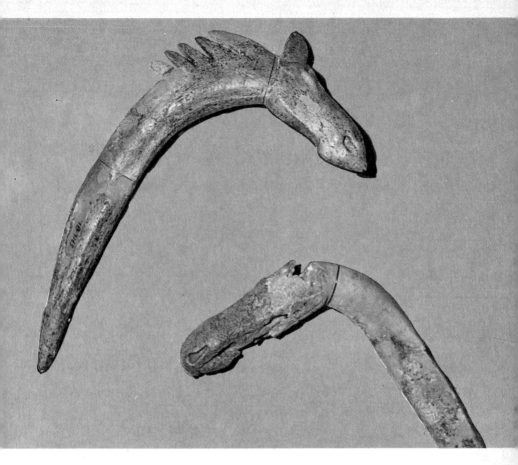

113, 114 Carvings of animals heads from the Arctic art group. *Above*, are two examples of the head and neck of an elk carved from bone found with a burial in the cemetery of Olen, Carelia. They were probably attached to a body made of skin stuffed with some filling material. *Below*, is a wooden ladle, the handle carved into the form of a naturalistic duck's head, from the Gorbunovo bog in the Central Urals

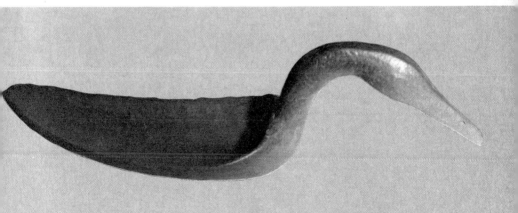

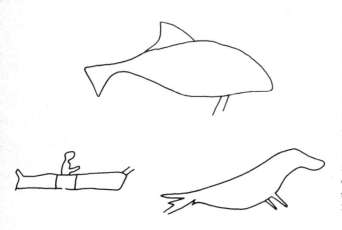

115–117 Means of transport have changed little in circumpolar regions since the Stone Age. *Left* is an Eskimo *umiak* covered by seal-skins. Note how the rigid members of the frame extend like ears at either end and note also the joins between the skins. The 'ears' may be clearly seen on a rock-engraving showing a man in a skin boat hunting a porpoise and a seal, from Bødøy, north-west Norway. *Below*, sledge transport is represented by a sledge-runner and a reconstruction of a complete wooden sledge of a kind used from Scandinavia to the Urals

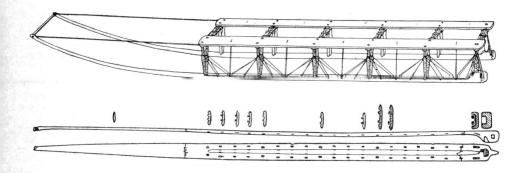

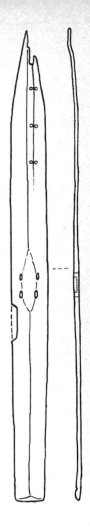

118, 119 Three skiers with their sticks are depicted on a rock-engraving in Carelia, on the river Vyg, and *right*, a wooden ski from the Stone Age of South Tavastland, Finland

generalized big-game hunting of an earlier age, in south-west Asia it was possible to continue to develop the close relations established with particular herds of game. In so far as there was any trend towards greater dryness at the crucial time this would only have lent greater impetus to the development of closer relations between groups of men and the animals on which they depended for an important element in their food; and by the same token it would have encouraged the more intensive gathering of whatever food-plants were available. Even if climatic change is entirely discounted, the mere fact that herd-hunting was able to continue without interruption in such territories as Palestine, the border lands of Iraq and Iran and the mountain regions overlooking the south-east Caspian must have favoured the closer relations that ultimately led by imperceptible gradations to the beginnings of domestication. Another reason why south-west Asia was so much favoured is that it happened to be the home of wild animals and plants particularly susceptible to domestication, notably sheep or goat and the cereals, emmer wheat and barley.

The economic transformation, which led to the establishment during the seventh millennium BC of formally Neolithic communities, that is communities based on farming, whose technology was founded on the use of flint and stone tools, including polished axes and adzes and who normally made pottery, marked only a further stage in the process of ensuring a more adequate supply of food that provides a main theme of prehistory. As we have seen, the earliest men emerged from a

120, 121 Slotted reaping-knife handle from Mugharet el-Kebarah, Palestine, *left*, and a diagrammatic view, *opposite*, showing flint insets of the kind that would have been set in such a handle. Flints used in such 'reaping' tools often show traces of silica gloss along their edge resulting from friction with the silica in cornstalks

predominantly vegetarian hominid stock through their prowess as hunters. Furthermore the archaeology of the Old Stone Age reflects prehistoric man's growing mastery in this field. Advanced Palaeolithic men, after all, were able to be more advanced primarily because of their use of hafted and complex hunting equipment. Another major step forward came with specialized herd-hunting. This in turn made possible incipient domestication with, in the fulness of time, selective breeding and the creation of a veritable bank of food, a bank able to supply the means by which civilization itself was able to arise in what is by the standards of prehistory only a brief period of time.

To describe the long-drawn-out process of domestication as a Revolution, as is sometimes done, is a plain misuse of words and to qualify as Neolithic a process which began during Palaeolithic times is merely perverse. It is surely more fitting to describe as a Transformation the process of increasing control from herd-hunting to incipient herding and full domestication and to ascribe it predominantly to the Transitional peoples who gradually modified the old Palaeolithic way of life, and whose transforming task was only ended with the emergence of the first societies that can properly be called Neolithic. When we examine the archaeological traces of the architects of the new way of life, it should be no surprise to find that they agree in broad outlines with those of the Transitional or Mesolithic peoples of Europe, whether in respect of the absence of pottery, the widespread use of microliths or the manufacture of specialized elements of bone equipment like barbless fish-hooks, barbed spear heads and equipment grooved or slotted for the reception of sharp flint blades. The achievement of Mesolithic man throughout the Advanced Palaeolithic world was in all essentials the same, namely to effect the transition from

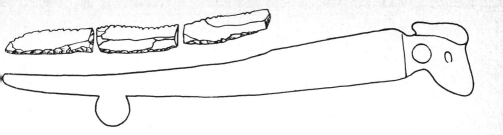

the age-old economy of hunting and gathering to that of farming. Yet we can recognize that in certain parts of south-west Asia his role was to make creative use of a unique set of circumstances, and in preparing the way for Neolithic peasants to lay the very foundations of urban, literate civilization.

Although study of their food refuse is still very incomplete, the animal bones from Natufian sites in the Mount Carmel caves and from the original encampment by the spring at the base of Tel-es-Sultan, Jericho, show a concentration on gazelle strong enough to suggest a special relationship with particular herds, comparable with that established by the Late Glacial reindeer-hunters of Europe. On the other hand stone mortars and pestles reflect the importance of plant food and bone reaping-knives set with flint blades showing signs of silica gloss suggest that cereal grasses were harvested. Whether these were wild or whether they had been modified or not by breeding we have no means of telling, because no samples have yet been studied. For present purposes it does not greatly matter; the important thing is that the Natufians had already concentrated on the harvesting of grasses sufficiently to develop what has proved to be the proto-type of all reaping instruments. Yet their artifacts as a whole are Mesolithic in character; they made numerous microliths, including a particular crescentic form having bipolar retouch at the back, as well as a variety of bone and antler tools such as barbed spearheads, barbless fish-hooks and slotted equipment. Again their art features animal and occasional anthropomorphic forms; and it is interesting that parts even of the gear used in reaping and pulverizing plant foods were carved into the forms of

Ills. 120, 121

122 Maglemo-sian, *left*, and Natu-fian, *right*, barbless bone fish-hooks

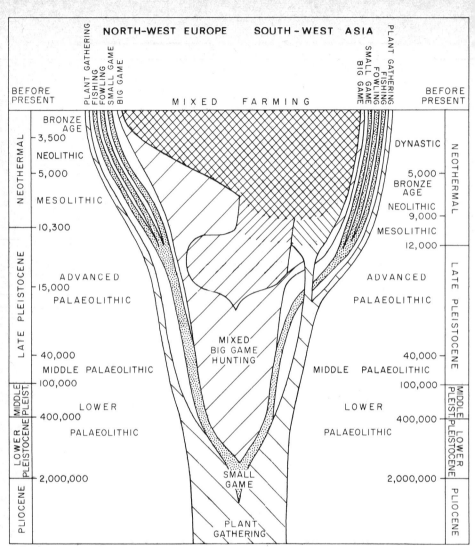

123 Chart showing in broad terms the evolution of the Primate food quest. The earliest men supplemented vegetable diet by small, easily caught game. The men of the Middle Pleistocene were already formidable big-game hunters. Before the end of the Late Pleistocene some groups of Advanced Palaeolithic men had begun to concentrate on particular herds, a process that ultimately led to their domestication. Plant foods began to be gathered with greater discrimination and special methods were evolved for harvesting the wild cereal grasses growing on the uplands of south-west Asia. No clear lines can be drawn in what was essentially a process of transformation from a parasitic to a production form of economy, but a crucial stage in the emergence of farming was evidently passed through in this area between twelve and nine thousand years ago. By c. 7000 BC the first recognizably Neolithic communities had emerged, marked by pottery and polished stone axes and securely based on a well-established mixed farming economy. It was in this form that the new way of life first spread to Europe

124 Upper part of a monumental circular funerary structure at Eynan beneath which was a total of nine burials. The plan is probably taken from the circular hut of the living, directly above which the tomb may have been built

wild animals, the bone handles of reaping-knives being terminated by animal-heads and stone pestles being shaped to the form of animal-hoofs.

Evidence both from burials and settlements suggest that the Natufians had managed to secure sufficient control of their food supply to increase in numbers and begin the process of settling down. As to burials, even in caves quite large cemeteries have been found – some 87 burials (64 adults) occurred at el Wad, 45 (28 adults) at Shouqbah; then in the extreme north of Israel at Eynan there is evidence of a monumental funerary structure built in the open on a circular plan with two layers of stone paving, the first covering remains of seven burials and the second of two more.

Ill. 124

Important evidence for the gradual transition to farming in the southern Levant is becoming available as open sites like Jericho and Beidha in Jordan and Nahal Oren in Israel are explored. Each of these have produced two archaeological assemblages overlying one of the classic Natufian kind long known from Shouqbah and el-Wad, namely aceramic A and B, which together equate in broad terms with the evolved Natufian or Tahounian of the Judaean caves. Aceramic A, associated with round or at least curvilinear structures, shows substantial continuity with classic Natufian, but the presence of Anatolian obsidian already points to influence from the north. In aceramic B, accompanied by rectangular buildings and the more general use of white plaster for floors and walls, northern influences make themselves more strongly felt, notably in the forms and mode of production of arrowheads. Analysis of organic materials or impressions of these from successive stages at such sites may be expected to throw increasing light on the transition from herding and specialized gathering to the level of domestication practised by formally Neolithic communities. Analysis of the goat remains from Beidha has shown that down to and including the classic Natufian occupation the bones of young animals were represented so much more strongly than in Palaeolithic assemblages from the same area as to suggest the beginnings of cultural control over livestock. Detailed information about cereals is so far available only from the aceramic B phase at Beidha. The evidence from cereal impressions suggests that an important threshold was being crossed. Barley was being cultivated but had not yet acquired all the characteristics of the domesticated form and emmer, though conforming morphologically to the definition of the cultivated variety, showed a range of variability often associated with plants in a stage of genetic transition.

The greater certainty of food supply made possible by herd management and cereal cultivation allowed a greater permanency of settlement and the aggregation of larger communities. Impressive evidence for this is provided by the massive defences comprising a rock-cut ditch with stone walls and bastion-like towers erected already by the aceramic A people round the original Natufian encampment at Tel-es-Sultan, Jericho. The material

125 Early Natufian house on virgin soil at Tel-es-Sultan, Jericho. The round, shallow pits in the floor were probably storage pits and the querns to the left indicate preparation of some form of plant foods, probably cereals

recovered from the series of deposits which accumulated, at this site between the first Natufian encampment and the appearance of pottery (*c*. 8–5000 BC) suggests that the population throughout this period was basically Natufian. In this connection it is indeed interesting that the earliest defenders of Tel-es-Sultan, the makers of hog's-back bricks, deposited the heads of their dead apart from the rest of the bodies, since this practice has been observed at the large Natufian tomb of Eynan. It is also significant from a broader point of view that head-burial was practised about the same time by the Meso-lithic inhabitants of part of South Germany, as seen most notably at Ofnet where nests of twenty-seven and five

Ills. 126–128

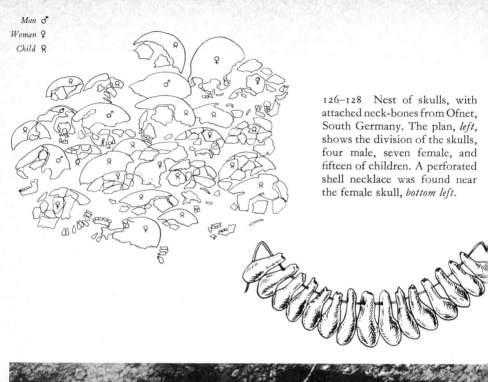

Man ♂
Woman ♀
Child ♀

126–128 Nest of skulls, with attached neck-bones from Ofnet, South Germany. The plan, *left*, shows the division of the skulls, four male, seven female, and fifteen of children. A perforated shell necklace was found near the female skull, *bottom left*.

129 Plastered skull with shells inset as eyes from Tel-es-Sultan, Jericho. This is only one of numerous examples found at the site

skulls with attached neck-bones were found coated with red ochre and accompanied by personal ornaments and a few microliths. The Tel-es-Sultan rite was more sophisticated in that the faces were modelled in clay and the eyes inset with shells, but the underlying similarity provides some confirmation at a psychic level of the broad community of culture that extended over the Mesolithic world from the Atlantic to the mountain zone of southwest Asia.

Ill. 129

Direct evidence about the sources of food of the community responsible for organizing the massive defences is unfortunately meagre but definite progress can be seen in the equipment used for grinding plant food and presumably mortars: the people who occupied oval houses made of hog's-back bricks and built the original defences made primitive querns; and those who followed, occupying houses with rectangular, plastered rooms, made a specialized form of quern with a grinding hollow that ran out at one end. How far the inhabitants of the walled town had carried the domestication of animals is

130, 131 The sharing of food and other essential commodities is one of the basic characteristics of human society. The scene, *above*, is of a Bushman distributing meat after a kill and *below*, a Bushman poisoning his arrows

also a matter of some speculation; one can only say for certain that the horn-cores of the goats seem to show some differences from wild ones. What the Jericho sequence undoubtedly shows is that the heirs of the Natufians managed somehow to ensure their sources of food to the point that made it possible to settle down in communities large enough and well enough disciplined to erect major defensive works and they did so without practising what have come to be regarded as the basic Neolithic arts of potting and weaving. The process of gaining control over sources of food was evidently a gradual one and it was achieved by people who were basically Mesolithic in culture.

To imagine that 'farming' was invented by any particular group is to misunderstand the whole process and in any case there is no reason to think that Palestine holds a special place in the vanguard of economic advance. As we have argued, the process of ensuring basic supplies of food underwent a marked acceleration with the developed hunting techniques introduced in the Advanced Palaeolithic world and in particular with the notion of establishing a special relationship with individual groups of wild animals during the final phase of the Pleistocene. With the hindsight of history we can now see that the Mesolithic hunter-fishers of the oak-pistachio zone of the Zagros and Taurus Mountains were particularly well placed because wild emmer, barley and goats existed in the habitat, all of them amenable to domestication.

The excavation of a stratified rock-shelter and a near-by prehistoric village settlement at Shanidar in northern Iraq, has given us a useful insight into the situation in this key region. Around 10000 BC the rock-shelter was apparently occupied by hunters specializing in wild goats. The most noticeable feature of their material equipment was an abundance of microliths, in many cases presumably intended to barb and tip arrows and including triangles,

Ill. 132

121

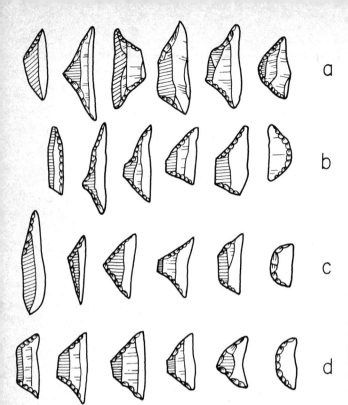

132 Microliths used to barb and tip projectile heads, from, *a* Star Carr, England; *b* La Cocina, Spain; *c* Palegawra, Iraq; *d* Jarmo, Iraq. These, together with barbed spearheads, slotted handles and hafts (*ills. 105, 120, 121*), barbless fish-hooks (*ill. 122*) and skull cults (*ills. 126–129*), point to a basic community among the cultures that bridged the gap between the Advanced Palaeolithic and Neolithic worlds from the Atlantic to western Asia

crescents and elongated trapezoidal forms, a constellation first recognized in the lower level at Palegawra, where once again it was associated with a hunting economy, the victims in this case including the gazelle and an equid as well as goat or wild sheep. In the following layer which reflected a drier climate and dated from the ninth millennium before Christ the same microlithic industry persisted, suggesting that the original population continued to occupy the site. Yet there are many signs that the inhabitants of the cave had by now made a decisive economic advance; querns as well as mortars and slotted reaping-knife handles with flint insets point to the harvesting and use of cereal crops and the changes in the ratio of age-groups and sexes among the goat or sheep clearly indicate herding and systematic butchery of young males with the maintenance of a high proportion of females for breeding and probably for milk and cheese as well. It is significant also that at this stage the Shanidar people were occupying villages in the open even if these were only seasonal; during the eighth millennium before Christ we know that the villagers of Jarmo in the same region, who made closely similar microliths and reaping-knives, were growing cultivated cereals and living in rectangular-roomed houses, though still not yet making pottery. The gap between the Advanced Hunters and the formally Neolithic pottery-making peasantries had indeed been bridged and in the archaeological record the people who bridged it betrayed their essentially Mesolithic character by microlithic industries of Palegawra type. Thus the Transitional or Mesolithic peoples uncon-sciously prepared the way for the next stage of prehistory: in favoured regions they accelerated processes which resulted in the appearance perhaps as early as 7000 B C of the earliest truly Neolithic pottery-making societies; and in marginal territories like north-west Europe lacking prototypes for domestic forms they were ready to absorb the new economy when it came.

CHAPTER SIX

Recent Hunters and Gatherers

So great was the advantage conferred by an economy
based on agriculture that hunter-fishers had been displaced
by farmers over all accessible and ecologically favoured
parts of the world long before the end of prehistoric
times. When Europeans began to open up the world they
found that communities based on the old way of life were
in the main confined to territories too cold, too dry or
too densely forested for the practice of agriculture or
horticulture under primitive conditions. Yet the arctic
and sub-arctic regions of northern Eurasia and North
America and the extreme tip of South America; the
Kalahari desert of South Africa; and the forests of
Amazonia, tropical Africa, Malaya, Sumatra, the Philip-
pines and the Celebes all afforded shelter to small communities of men who lived to all intents and purposes at
the same level of technology as the Mesolithic peoples of
north-west Europe between five and ten thousand years
ago. Even more interesting in some respects was the
situation encountered in Australia, originally colonized,
probably between twelve and twenty thousand years ago,
at a time when ocean levels were substantially lower than
at the present time, but subsequently cut off from easy
access by rising sea-levels. Geographical remoteness, the
archaic nature of its vegetation and animal life and the

133 Bushman testing the resilience and tension of his bow

conservatism of its inhabitants bred by millennia of isolation all helped to insulate the continent from the outer world. Impulses certainly reached Australia from Indonesia and New Guinea as early as the third millennium before Christ, but horticulture already practised at this time in the highlands of New Guinea failed to penetrate the continent, which was also by-passed by the great migrations responsible for spreading pig-breeding and garden cultivation over the Pacific islands. The aborigines who greeted Captain Phillip and his fleet of convict ships as they anchored in Sydney Cove in January 1788 by setting up 'a horrid howl and indicat[ing] by angry gestures with sticks and stones that the white man was not wanted' were heirs of a long indigenous tradition, but this tradition, modified though it was by influences from the north, was ultimately Palaeolithic in essence.

None of these peoples have contributed to the main line of human history except in the most marginal way and, with the hindsight of history, we might be tempted to dismiss them as of little consequence. Yet it would be wrong and unpardonably arrogant to think of them as peoples who might as well not have existed. These peoples after all utilized environments that were still inaccessible – and still are to some degree – to economically and technologically more advanced ones. In this sense they were biologically successful and they achieved success with a store of social capital so meagre as to compel admiration rather than condescension. In the last analysis they are not in need of praise or blame: they claim our interest because they show how men are able to live under extreme conditions with only the slightest technical know-how by depending on wild products. And they help us to understand more fully the kind of limitations under which our own forebears nevertheless achieved fulfilment in the age-long period before food-production had begun to lay a secure basis for the more advanced civilization of man.

The limitations were sufficiently real. First there is the brute fact of demography: the density of population, the area of ground needed to support an individual and the size of community in which men were able habitually to live, is controlled more or less strictly by the productivity and above all by the reliability of the supply of food. *Ills. 130, 131* Under certain rather special conditions, it is true, plentiful and assured supplies may be available up to a point to peoples dependent on hunting and catching. Seasonal runs of salmon up some of the rivers of the Pacific coast of North America allow certain groups of Indians to obtain most of the protein they need in the course of a few weeks and this enables them to live in quite large communities, build substantial wooden houses and even institutionalize the display and destruction of wealth as a means of acquiring social esteem. Yet even under the most favourable conditions there is a limit to the scale and permanence of communities based on catching activities. As we have seen, specialized gazelle or goat hunting and the harvesting of wild grasses likewise allowed communities in restricted parts of south-west Asia to begin the process of settling down some nine or ten thousand years ago; but, significantly, it was not until sheep or goat and cereals had been tamed and their reproduction regulated that formal Neolithic culture was able to emerge as a platform for a rapid development of the arts of literate civilization. It is a matter of observation that with few exceptions peoples depending on hunting and gathering need much more extensive territories for their support than those practising more advanced forms of economy. Precise figures can rarely be quoted, but to give some notion of what is meant by a low density of population one may recall that ethnologists have estimated that Tasmania, a country rather more than half the size of England and Wales, was occupied only by two to five thousand aborigines at the time of the English settlement; and that the whole continent of Australia, only fractionally smaller than the United States without Alaska, supported no more than some three hundred

134 Australian aborigine finishing off a *woomera* with a stone tool. Note how he uses his heel to hold it steady

thousand divided into five or six hundred language groups.

People unable to produce their own food at will had perforce to seek natural harvests and this meant that they had to move over an extensive territory, systematically gathering fruits, roots, shoots or eggs in their due seasons, following game and, where local conditions allowed, supplementing these terrestial sources by fishing and gathering shell fish. To follow such a life successfully implies an accurate knowledge of seasonal changes in animals and plants and of their various potentialities, a knowledge reflected in both the behaviour and vocabulary of peoples like the aborigines of Arnhem Land or the

135 Australian aborigine adding resin to the end of his *woomera* to hold the stone blade (*cf. ill. 85*)

western desert of Australia whose technology and way of life appears to us to be so primitive. The need to move over extensive territories in pursuit of food also implies a knowledge of how to find water, and travellers in the Kalahari or the central Australian desert regions know well how skilled the aboriginal peoples are in this respect. There is much to admire in the ability of the Bushmen or Australians in finding food and drink in territories that might appear to us so forbidding. The fact remains that the necessity to wander over wide tracts imposes narrow limits on cultural advance. It means that a man may own few possessions – an Australian aboriginal man's main capital is the bunch of spears, throwing stick and

Ill. 133
Ills. 136, 137

Ills. 83, 134, 135

136, 137 Digging sticks are an essential part of an Australian aborigine's basic equipment along with his spear and his *woomera*, which has many uses not least as a spear-thrower. *Left*, an aborigine is testing the working end of his digging-stick and *opposite*, an aborigine child uses one rapidly to dig a hole

spear-thrower-cum-shield-cum-carrier (*woomera*) that he normally carries around. Equally, it implies more or less frequent changes of camp and this in itself inhibits the rise of anything like settled communities. As a rule the natural shelters of overhanging rocks and caves serve for his home or alternatively windbreaks or huts made of bark or grass laid over light frames of bent branches serve in warmer climates or some form of earth-house in colder ones.

Ills. 30, 69

The need for seasonal movement and the fact that hunter-fishers have in general to live in communities too small to allow of any significant sub-division of labour beyond that imposed by age or sex have between them prevented the emergence of any elaborate technology. People with this pattern of subsistence rely for their tools, weapons, containers and other equipment on natural

substances shaped by simple means to the required form
or used directly as they are. Until, like the Bushmen, they
came into contact with peoples using iron, hunter-
fishers have always had to rely on flint or stone for
shaping other raw materials. In remote parts of Australia
this has persisted down to modern times. When, as if to
symbolize the triumph of modern technology, telephone
lines were carried across the northern parts of the continent, the aborigines profited in the only way they knew
by breaking off the insulators and using them as raw
material for flaking their spearheads; and this could only   *Ill. 50*
be remedied by leaving deposits of bottle glass, an even
more desirable raw material, at the foot of the poles. No
one who has visited great ethnographic collections like
those at the British Museum or the Pitt-Rivers Museum,
Oxford, or, better still, has handled the weapons of an

Australian aborigine can doubt the capabilities of flint and stone in shaping wood and other organic materials. Again, though few of us would care to get through the day without using glass, pottery or metal containers, it must not be supposed that primitive man made do with his bare hands. Apart from natural forms like gourds, shells or even leaves that might be used directly, effective containers are made by modern peoples of simple culture by sewing skins, plaiting grasses and fibres or carving wood. In judging material equipment one has always to take account of the circumstances and needs to which it was adapted and in this respect the productions of primitive man are not inferior to our own.

Yet it is hardly possible to view human society outside its historical context. However successful the culture of an Arnhemlander or a Bindibu is considered as a quasi-biological mechanism – and we have always to remember that the lowest animals survive and flourish in their appropriate environmental niches without even a trace of culture – the fact remains that more complex societies, involving an ever greater subdivision of labour and social function, could only emerge because certain groups of prehistoric men transformed the basis of their food-supply and crossed the threshold of systematic agriculture and stock-raising. How far modern man is right to equate greater complexity with progress, in any absolute sense is a question for philosophers. One certain way in which he has advanced over his primitive forebears, let alone over other animals, is in his capacity to range widely over time. He betrays his superiority as much in his quest for his own prehistory as in his exploration of outer space and his plans for his own future.

Bibliography

ANATI, E. *Palestine before the Hebrews.* London, 1963.
BADER, O. N. *La Caverne Kapovaïa. Peinture paléolithique.* Moscow, 1965
BRAIDWOOD, R. J., and HOWE, B. *Prehistoric Investigations in Iraqui Kurdistan.* Chicago, 1960.
BUTZER, K. W. *Environment and Archaeology.* Chicago, 1964.
BRONDSTED, J. *Danmarke Oldtid* I. 2nd ed. Copenhagen, 1957.
CLARK, G. *World Prehistory.* Cambridge, reprinted 1965.
—— and PIGGOTT, S. *Prehistoric Societies.* London, 1965.
CLARK, J. D. *The Prehistory of Southern Africa.* Harmondsworth, 1959.
COLE, S. *The Prehistory of East Africa.* Harmondsworth, 1954.
FORDE, D. *Habitat, Economy and Society.* 4th ed. London, 1961.
GARROD, D. A. D., and CLARK, J. G. D. *Primitive Man in Egypt, Western Asia and Europe.* Fascicle 30, *Cambridge Ancient History.* Revised ed. 1965.
GRAZIOSI, P. *Palaeolithic Art.* London, 1960.
HAWKES, J., and WOOLLEY, SIR LEONARD. *Prehistory and the Beginning of Civilization.* London, 1963.
KIRKBRIDE, D. 'Five Seasons at the Pre-pottery Neolithic Village of Beidha in Jordan', *Palestine Exploration Quarterly,* January–June 1966, 8–72.
LAMING, A. *Lascaux: Paintings and Engravings.* Harmondsworth, 1959.
LAMING-EMPERAIRE, A. *La Signification de l'art paléolithique.* Paris, 1962.
LEAKEY, L. S. B. *Adam's Ancestors.* 4th ed. London, 1953.
LE GROS CLARK, SIR WILFRED. *The Fossil Evidence for Human Evolution.* 2nd ed. Chicago, 1964.
LEROI-GOURHAN, A. *Préhistoire de l'art occidental.* Paris, 1965.
MARSHALL, J. 'Man as a Hunter', *Natural History,* June–July and August–September 1958. American Museum of Natural History, New York.
MCBURNEY, C. B. M. *The Stone Age of Northern Africa.* Harmondsworth, 1960.
—— *Haua Fteah and the Stone Age of the South-east Mediterranean.* Cambridge, 1967.
MCCARTHY, F. D. *Australian Aborigines; their Life and Culture.* Melbourne, 1957.
MONGAIT, A. L. *Archaeology in the U.S.S.R.* Harmondsworth, 1961.
OAKLEY, K. P. *Man the Tool-maker.* British Museum (Natural History). 3rd ed. London, 1956.
—— *Frameworks for Dating Fossil Man.* London, 1964.
SOLECKI, R. S. 'Prehistory in Shanidar Valley, Northern Iraq', *Science,* vol. 139, no. 1551, 179–93. New York, 1963.
THOMSON, D. F. 'Some wood and stone implements of the Bindibu tribe of Central West Australia', *Proc. Prehist. Soc.* XXX(1964), 400–22.
TOBIAS, P. 'New Discoveries in Tanganyika, their bearing on Hominid Evolution', *Current Anthropology,* vol. 6, 391 ff. Chicago, 1965.
WASHBURN, S. L. *Social Life of Early Man.* London, 1962.

List of Illustrations

The author and publishers are grateful to the many official bodies and institutions mentioned below for their assistance in supplying illustration material. Illustrations without acknowledgement are from originals in Thames and Hudson's archives. Special gratitude is expressed to Professor Tage Ellinger of Copenhagen for photographs taken in the Hermitage Museum, Leningrad; to Professor Donald Thomson of Melbourne University for photographs of the Australian Bindubi people; to Mr Axel Poignant for his photographs of Australian aborigines in Arnhem Land; and to Mrs Laurence K. Marshall of Boston for her great kindness in making available photographs of Bushmen taken by her late husband, Mr John Marshall.

Museum (Natural History). Photo Peter Clayton

2 Male burial, *Homo neanderthalensis*, from Mugharet-es-Skhūl, Mount Carmel. Drawn by Philip Ward after Garrod

3 Burial of a Neanderthal boy from Teshik-Tash, Uzbekistan. Drawn by Lucinda Rodd after Okladnikov

4 Skull of *Homo sapiens* from Cro-Magnon, Dordogne. Drawn by M. Maitland Howard after Boule and Vallois

5 Stone implements from lower level at Kenniff cave, Queensland. After Mulvaney

6 Map of the Advanced Palaeolithic world. Drawn by Charles Hasler

7, 28 Advanced Paleolithic blade tools from La Madeleine. Museum of Archaeology and Ethnology, Cambridge

9 Antlers exhibiting groove and splinter technique. Museum of Archaeology and Ethnology, Cambridge

10 Rock-shelter, Devon Downs, Adelaide, Australia. Photo the author

11 Mammoth hunters' dwelling, South Russia. Reconstruction after Mongait

12 Round hut-floor and mammoth tusks, Dolní Věstonice, Czechoslovakia. Photo courtesy of Dr B. Klíma

13 Flint implements of the Dabba culture. Drawn by Lucinda Rodd after the author

14 Aurignacian flints. After Oakley

15 Split-base bone point, from the Istálló-sköer Höhle, Hungary. Drawn by Lucinda Rodd after Vértes

16 Gravettian hunters' rubbish dump of bones. Dolní Věstonice, Czechoslovakia. Photo courtesy of Dr B. Klíma

37 Gravettian flint-work from Romanelli, Italy. Drawn by Lucinda Rodd after Blanc

38, 39 Baked clay mixture female figurine from Dolní Věstonice. Brno Museum. Photo J. Kleibl

40 Mammoth tusk stylized female figurine from Dolní Věstonice. Brno Museum. Photo J. Kleibl

41 Ivory female head from Brassempouy, Landes. National Museum, St Germain-en-Laye. Photo A. Leroi-Gourhan

42, 43 Ivory female figurine from Lespugue, Haute-Garonne. Musée de l'Homme, Paris. Photos R. Pasquino and J. Vertut

44 Haematite female torso from Ostrava-Petřkovice, Czechoslovakia. Archaeological Institute, Brno

45 Stylized woman engraved on mammoth ivory from Předmostí, Czechoslovakia. Brno Museum. Photo J. Kleibl

46–48 Mammoth bone female figurine from Site I, Kostienki, South Russia. Photos courtesy of Professor Tage Ellinger

49 Solutrean laurel leaf point from Le Solutré. British Museum. Photo courtesy of the Trustees of the British Museum

50 Flaked bottle glass spearhead, North Australia. Museum of Archaeology and Ethnology, Cambridge

51 Reindeer skeleton from Villestofte, Denmark. National Museum, Copenhagen

52–4 Late Magdalenian harpoon heads. After Leroi-Gourhan and Oakley

55, 56 Reindeer antler spear-thrower from Mas d'Azil. Collection Péquart, St Brieuc. Photo Archives, drawing by Hubert Pepper

57 Reproduction of cave paintings of

137

mammoths, Kapovaya cave, southern Urals. Photo courtesy of Professor Tage Ellinger

58 Abstract finger drawings in red clay. La Baume Latrone, Gard. Photo B. Pell

59 Engraved bison, La Grèze, Dordogne. Photo J. Vertut

60 Engraving of a young deer, Levanzo, Sicily. Photo B. Graziosi

61 Standing bison engraved on a pebble from Laugerie Basse, Dordogne. Musée de l'Homme, Paris. From a cast in the Institute of Archaeology, London. Photo Peter Clayton

62 Engraving of a vulva in Style I, La Ferrassie, Dordogne

63 Limestone relief sculpture, Le Roc de Sers, Charente. Photo Archives

64 Painted horse in Style IV, Le Portel, Ariège

65 Painted black bison in Style III, Lascaux, Dordogne. Photo Peter Bellew

66 Table of sexual symbols in cave art. Drawn by Lucinda Rodd after Leroi-Gourhan

67 Australian aborigine painting a design on bark. Photo Axel Poignant

68 Negative hand outlines, Gargas, Hautes Pyrénées. Photo J. Vertut

69 Negative hand outlines, Toombs, New South Wales. Photo Dermot A. Casey

70 Limestone relief, the Venus of Laussel. Photo J. Vertut

71 Symbolic design, Castillo, Santander. Photo B. Pell

72 Bison engraved on clay, Niaux. Photo J. Vertut

73 Deer painted on the ceiling, Altamira, Santander. Photo J. Vertut

74 Hunter and leaping ibex, painting, Remigia, Gasulla. From a copy by Douglas Mazonowicz, Editions Alecto

75 Stag antler mask from Star Carr, Yorkshire. British Museum (Natural History). Photo courtesy of the Trustees of the British Museum

76 Tungu shaman. After N. Witsen, *Noorden Oost Tartarye*, Amsterdam, 1705

77 Painting of a ritual postulant, St Vidgeon, Arnhem Land. Photo G. Donkin

78, 79 The 'sorcerer', Les Trois Frères, Ariège. Drawing by Diana Holmes after Breuil. Photo J-D Lajoux

80 Magdalenian needles and pendants. Museum of Archaeology and Ethnology, Cambridge

81 Skull with shell ornament, Grotte des Enfants, Grimaldi. Musée d'Anthropologie de Monaco

82 Wooden bows from Holmegard, Denmark. National Museum, Copenhagen

83 Australian aborigine family on the move. Photo Axel Poignant

84 Forepart and base of a wooden arrowshaft from Vinkelmose, Denmark. National Museum, Copenhagen

85 Forepart of an arrow from Løshult, Sweden. Lund Historical Museum

86 Danish shell mound. National Museum, Copenhagen

87 Aborigine shell mound, Australia. Photo Axel Poignant

88 Australian aborigine throwing a spear. Photo Axel Poignant

89 Stag antler barbed spearhead from the North Sea. Norwich Castle Museum

90 Australian aborigine spear fishing. Photo Axel Poignant

91 Plaited fish-trap from Holbaek, Jutland. National Museum, Copenhagen

92 Pine bark floats and bast net fragments from Korpilahti, Antrea, Finland. Photo after S. Pälsi

93 Felled birch trees, Star Carr, Yorkshire. Photo Walker

94 Mattock of elk antler from Star Carr, Yorkshire. Drawn by Philip Ward after the author

95 Flint adze-head in antler sleeve from Svaedborg. National Museum, Copenhagen. Photo Sophus Bergtsson

96 Wooden paddle from Duvensee, Schleswig-Holstein. Drawn by Philip Ward after Schwantes

97 Pine trunk dug-out canoe from Pesse, Drenthe. Provincial Museum van Drenthe, Assen. Photo Biologisch-Archaeologisch Instituut, University of Groningen

98 Maglemose amber carvings from Denmark. National Museum, Copenhagen

99, 100 Decorated stag antler mattock, with expanded drawing, from Jordløse Denmark. National Museum, Copenhagen. Drawn by Philip Ward

101 Engraved wild ox bone from Ryemarkgård, Zealand. National Museum, Copenhagen

102 Sacred stones being shown to initiates, Arnhem Land. Photo Axel Poignant

103 Painted pebbles from Mas d'Azil, Ariège. Drawn by Philip Ward after Piette

104 Hollow ground axe of Circumpolar type. Museum of Archaeology and Ethnology, Cambridge

105 Slotted spearhead with flint insets from Bussjö mosse, Scania, Sweden. State Historical Museum, Stockholm

106 Plan of stone-lined male grave, Téviec, Morbihan. Drawn by Philip Ward after Péquart

107 Comb and pit marked pot from Carelia. Drawn by Lucinda Rodd after Gimbutas

108 Engraving of a reindeer beside a waterfall at Böla, Nord-Tröndelag, Norway. Photo courtesy of Professor S. Marstrander

109 Bone harpoon head from Norrköping, Sweden. State Historical Museum, Stockholm

110 Reindeer branding in Lapland. Photo courtesy of the Swedish Travel Association.

111 Elk hunt carving, Nämforsen, Norrland, Sweden. Photo courtesy of Dr S. Janson

112 Stone mace-head from Hvittis, Finland. National Museum, Helsinki

113 Carved bone elk heads from Olen, Carelia. Photo courtesy of Professor Tage Ellinger

114 Wooden ladle with duck-head handle from Gorbunovo, Central Urals. Photo courtesy of Professor Tage Ellinger

115 Eskimo *umiak*. Photo Jette Bang, courtesy of the Artic Institut, Charlottenlund, Denmark

116 Rock engraving, Bødøy, north-west Norway. Drawn by Lucinda Rodd after the author

117 Reconstruction of a Stone Age sledge. After the author

118 Rock engraving of three skiers, river Vyg. After Ravdonikas and Gimbutas

119 Wooden ski from South Tavastland, Finland. National Museum, Helsingfors

120, 121 Bone sickle-shaft from Mugharet el-Kebarah. Amman Museum

122 Maglemosian and Natufian bone fish-hooks. After the author

123 Chart of the evolution of the Primate food quest. Drawn by Lucinda Rodd after the author

124 The great tomb, Eynan, Israel. Photo courtesy of Dr Jean Perrot and the Department of Antiquities, Israel

125 Early Natufian house with storage pits, Jericho. Photo courtesy of the British School of Archaeology in Jerusalem

126–128 Group of skulls from Ofnet, Bavaria, with key and reconstructed shell necklace. Photo after R. R. Schmidt, drawings by Diana Holmes

129 Human skull with plaster modelling and inset shell eyes from Jericho.

Amman Museum. Photo courtesy of the British School of Archaeology in Jerusalem

130 Bushmen sharing meat. Photo courtesy of Mrs L. Marshall

131 Bushman poisoning arrowheads. Photo courtesy of Mrs L. Marshall

132 Microliths of Europe and south-west Asia. Drawn by Lucinda Rodd

133 Bushman testing his bow. Photo courtesy of Mrs L. Marshall

134 Australian aborigine finishing off a *woomera*. Photo courtesy of Professor Donald Thomson

135 Australian aborigine adding resin to his *woomera*. Photo courtesy of Professor Donald Thomson

136 Australian aborigine testing a digging stick. Photo courtesy of Professor Donald Thomson

137 Australian aborigine child grubbing with a digging stick. Photo Axel Poignant

Index

Numbers in italics refer to illustrations